WAGNER
DIE WALKÜRE

Hildegard Behrens · Jessye Norman · Christa Ludwig
Gary Lakes · James Morris · Kurt Moll
The Metropolitan Opera Orchestra
JAMES LEVINE

Now available on CDs and cassettes at record stores nationwide.
CDs: 423 389-2 GH4
MCs: 423 389-4 GH3

"…the Metropolitan Opera Orchestra are one of the stars of this performance. The playing is always secure, but goes beyond mere confidence into a gloriously exciting projection of the score's multifarious combinations of colours, nurtured by Levine to produce a richness of detail unsurpassed in any other recording."

(Gramophone, November 1988)

In music and in banking — imagination is the key.

One of the leading banks in the world.

Dresdner Bank

In USA: New York, Chicago, Los Angeles, Houston, Miami.

THE RING

METROPOLITAN OPERA

Published by the Metropolitan Opera Guild, Inc.

Das Rheingold, Scene 1: Alberich (Franz Mazura) steals the Rhinegold

*Das Rheingold, Scene 4: Donner (Gregg Baker), Fricka (Hanna Schwarz), Freia (Ellen Shade), Froh (Mark W. Baker)
and Wotan (Hans Sotin) prepare to cross a rainbow bridge to Valhalla, new home of the gods*

DER RING DES NIBELUNGEN

(The Ring of the Nibelung)
Cycle of four music dramas
Music and Libretto by Richard Wagner

Das Rheingold — Die Walküre
Siegfried — Götterdämmerung

Conductor: James Levine
Production: Otto Schenk
Set and projection design: Günther Schneider-Siemssen
Costume design: Rolf Langenfass
Lighting design: Gil Wechsler

FORGERS OF THE RING

BRUCE CRAWFORD
General Manager

The concept for the new Metropolitan Opera production of Der Ring des Nibelungen is particularly right for this time and this house. It is a magnificent combination of a traditional way of treating the story as myth, at the same time employing the stagecraft we have today. This is our own Ring for this particular theater. As one hears the final chords of Götterdämmerung, the overwhelming feeling I have is how successful and worthwhile the project has been.

JAMES LEVINE
Music Director

Today more than ever, the greatest enemies to the presentation of Wagner are superficiality and a distorting eccentricity. The hardest task of all is to present any masterpiece in a way that is faithful to all the facets of its specific identity, while also giving a modern audience an experience as close as possible to what would have been felt by the public at the time it was composed. We want the audience to get close to the composer's personality by putting all our resources at his disposal.

OTTO SCHENK
Producer

You should recognize the behavior of the Ring characters as timeless—their reactions to might, love, greed, anger and killing. With new types of light and stage treatment, we want to tell an old story in a very human and passionate way—
the way I think Wagner wanted it to be.

GÜNTHER SCHNEIDER-SIEMSSEN
Set Designer

This is my sixth production of Der Ring des Nibelungen, and for me it is a way of expressing something of the New Romanticism. The technology available at the Met is fantastic, and with the possibilities of movement and transformation, the visual and musical elements can be absolutely together. I think the U.S. in the space age is part of the New Romanticism, and the theater must go in the same direction.

ROLF LANGENFASS
Costume Designer

It is best to let the singers become the image, to help them rather than overburden them with fussy or elaborate costumes, which will disturb artists and spectators. You look at these characters for an endless time, and anything that is overdesigned or imposed will look false. There can be nothing phony in Wagner. One has to keep the ridiculous out of it and let the emotions and music work.

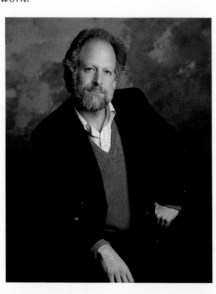

GIL WECHSLER
Lighting Designer

The challenge for the lighting director in our production is to create the magical effects Wagner calls for—fire, water, storm, sunrise, sunset, the supernatural and the earthly. They have to appear and disappear more rapidly than in real life, and during these fast transitions, we have to conceal the elaborate mechanics.

THE EVOLUTION OF THE RING

by Barry Millington

When, in 1848, Richard Wagner began to map out his first plan for *Der Ring des Nibelungen,* he was an ambitious young composer of revolutionary inclinations, ready to man the barricades of Dresden. Twenty-six years later, as he put the finishing touches to the score of *Götterdämmerung,* an enormous amount had changed. Wagner himself was an aging, somewhat disillusioned man, and his outlook had evolved in tune with the altered political face of his native Germany. No attempt to come to grips with the central masterpiece of Wagner's life work can afford to ignore the developing world view of its creator over the period of its germination and execution.

By 1848 Wagner had become convinced that so long as art was associated with capitalist speculation and profit making, no works of lasting value or true artistic integrity could be produced. Contemporary opera, he considered, was frivolous and superficial, mere entertainment for a degenerate bourgeoisie. Looking back to what he saw as the ideal form of art, the Greek drama, Wagner prescribed a modern equivalent in which the individual media of music, poetry and dance, in conjunction with the arts of architecture, sculpture and painting, could be restored to their true stature within a united art work. The new drama would be conceived and executed by not a single creative artist but a fellowship of artists. Traditional theaters, with their blatant social distinctions, would necessarily give way to structures designed to enhance beauty and intelligibility. Stage sets would be painted by genuine landscape artists. The drama would be enacted by the "actor of the future"—musician, poet and dancer in one.

This concept of the *Gesamtkunstwerk* (total work of art) did not originate with Wagner: it had been advocated in different forms by various prominent writers before him. Similarly, the call for a return to the Greek ideal was something of a commonplace. Even the idea of the creation of a national opera that would articulate the sentiments of the German people ripe for revolution had been put forward by Franz Brendel, editor of the influential periodical *Neue Zeitschrift für Musik,* in 1845-46. Brendel and others actually had proposed the Nibelung legend as subject for such an opera, and in 1845 Brendel had issued the following exhortation: "In my view a setting of the Nibelung opera would indeed be a step forward, and I believe the composer who could accomplish this task in an adequate manner would become the man of his era." Did Wagner recognize himself as this man of destiny?

At a time when he had made but a few sketches for what was to become the *Ring*, Wagner wrote to his friend Ernst Benedikt Kietz (September 14, 1850) that he was unable to reconcile himself to the idea of trusting to luck and having the eventual work performed "by the very first theater that comes along." On the contrary, he continued, he was toying with a bold plan to have "a theater erected here on the spot, made of planks, and have the most suitable singers join me here, and arrange everything necessary for this one special occasion, so that I could be certain of an outstanding performance of the opera." He would send out invitations to all interested in his works and "give three performances—free, of course—one after the other, in the space of a week, after which the theater would be demolished and the whole affair would be over and done with."

This utopian vision remained with Wagner throughout the quarter century of his work on the *Ring*, and in a pair of letters to Friedrich Feustel, leader of the town council of Bayreuth (November 1871 and April 1872), shortly after that town had been chosen as an ideal location for the enterprise. Wagner showed every intention of adhering to the original conception, albeit with a few minor alterations. The theater was still to be a provisional structure, possibly of wood, but was subsequently to be handed over to the nation. The festival was to be strictly nonprofit, the performances to be attended only by invited guests and "patrons" (i.e., sponsors), with no admission charges and a number of seats distributed free to residents of Bayreuth; singers and instrumentalists were to receive expenses only, no fees. Wagner struggled hard to realize his vision, and accepted compromises only with reluctance. Vestiges of the original scheme still remain today, notably the wooden seats, but to bring the project to fruition Wagner was compelled finally to rely on a scheme of patrons' certificates, which inevitably restricted admission to an affluent, privileged section of society. Over a century later, that restriction is, if anything, tighter than ever.

In taking up the Nibelung story, Wagner was providing himself with a rich fund of saga and epic material from the twelfth and thirteenth centuries. Two years earlier, he had been contemplating, even sketching, a five-act work on the twelfth-century emperor Frederick Barbarossa. According to autobiographical accounts in *A Communication to my Friends* and *My Life*, he abandoned that historical subject as soon as the greater potential of the Nibelung myth dawned on him. We now know that such was not the case: *Friedrich I* was evidently still in his mind after the completion of the libretto of *Siegfrieds Tod* (Siegfried's Death)—which later became *Götterdämmerung*—in December 1848, as is clear from the existence of a late sketch for the second act of the former. Moreover, it has now also come to light that the essay called *The Wibelungen: World History out of Saga* was written not before *Siegfrieds Tod* (and its initial prose résumé, *The Nibelungen Myth as Sketch for a Drama*) but after. The interesting thing about *The Wibelungen* is that it weaves together the historical story of Frederick Barbarossa with the legendary one of the Nibelungen. Contrary to Wagner's claims to have recognized immediately the potentiality of "pure" myth, the historical roots of his conception were evident until a surprisingly late stage.

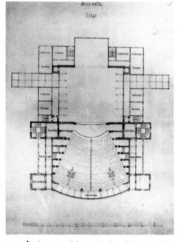

Architectural design by Otto Brückwald for Wagner's custom-made Festival Theater in Bayreuth, the auditorium of which is not a horseshoe but fan-shaped; construction began in 1872

t is not always fully appreciated to what extent Wagner drew on the Greek tragedians for the dramatic content of his work. From Aeschylus' *Oresteia*, which he had been reading avidly in the summer of 1847, he took not only the structure of a trilogy (*Das Rheingold* was merely a "preliminary evening") but also the linking themes of guilt and a curse. The confrontation of pairs of characters, a feature of the *Ring*, also recalls the *Oresteia*, and it even has been suggested that Aeschylus' use of recurrent imagery influenced Wagner's evolution of the leitmotif principle. But it is the *Prometheus* trilogy—now thought probably not to be the work of Aeschylus—that offers the closest parallels to the *Ring* in terms of character and dramatic situation. Brünnhilde and Prometheus are both offspring of an earth goddess who has the gift of prophecy; both defy the ruler of the gods and are punished by being bound on a rock by a fire god; both foretell to a woman that her descendants will perform heroic deeds; both are freed by a hero. No wonder Wagner was later to say of his classical awakening at this period, "My ideas about the significance of drama, and particularly of the theater, were decisively molded by these impressions."

The fact that the *Ring* draws so extensively on myth, both Greek and Norse, does not prevent it from being rooted firmly in the historical conditions prevailing at the time of its creation. The social and political dimension of the cycle, far from restricting its accessibility and relevance to subsequent generations, are intertwined with its supposedly timeless mythological content. Siegfried may be the archetypal, dragon-slaying hero, but he is also, as George Bernard Shaw put it, the naive anarchist who will overturn religion, law and order to free humanity from its fetters. Alberich may be the classic misbegotten dwarf of myth and legend, but he is also, in Shaw's terms, the plutocrat, the capitalist who exploits enslaved workers to increase his own wealth.

Until the various politically oriented productions of the *Ring* seen in the last two decades, notably that of Patrice Chéreau at Bayreuth, it often was accepted unthinkingly that the universality of Wagner's message eclipsed such allegorical intentions as Shaw proposed. Yet it is clear from Wagner's writings and letters of the period, and from comments recorded later in Cosima's diaries, that the *Ring* did reflect a powerful surge of socialist zeal. The revolution came and went, however, without noticeably transforming either the hearts and minds of the populace or the material conditions of their existence. Nor did it do anything to create a ready audience for the "art work of the future"—quite the reverse, in fact, as Wagner was obliged to retreat into exile, where he remained for over a decade, far from the public eye. Nationalist aspirations eventually were resolved by the unification of the German states in the Second Reich, proclaimed in January 1871, but as the creation of the conservative Bismarck, this was quite far removed from the idealistic vision of the 1840s. By 1871, Wagner's attitude toward politicians of all colors was one of cynicism and despair, and it scarcely came as a surprise to him that the Reich offered so little assistance when, in the 1870s, the Bayreuth project appeared to be collapsing.

The audience that eventually flocked to the Festspielhaus when it opened its doors in August 1876 was a far cry from the *Volk*, the German common people, that Wagner had anticipated so enthusiastically in his early days. It was in fact a well-heeled bourgeoisie, which derived little pleasure from the contemplation of a radically restructured society. And Wagner himself, with the passing years, was not the same man. Critical acclamation, social esteem, material security—indeed relative prosperity—and ripeness of years all conspired to color his outlook. Though he remained something of an idealist, he no longer expected or probably desired to see society fundamentally transformed, at least not in economic terms.

All this, naturally, is reflected in the *Ring*. But Wagner's sociopolitical evolution over its period of creation was paralleled by a changing philosophical perspective. In the prerevolutionary decade of the 1840s, he was profoundly influenced, as were many contemporary intellectuals and artists, by the ideas of Ludwig Feuerbach (1804-72). For Feuerbach, the essence of human nature and the source of its morality was the "I–you" relationship. Morality was inconceivable for the solitary being; only in conjunction with another, by creating a mutual drive to happiness, did an individual develop any consciousness of social responsibility. Feuerbach's elevation of love over material possessions, over everything, found expression in the revised ending that Wagner made in 1851 for *Siegfrieds Tod*: "Not wealth, not gold, nor godly splendor; not house, not court, nor overbearing pomp;... blessed in joy and

Above: Leopold Damrosch, friend of Wagner and the conductor who first introduced a Ring music drama into the repertory of the Metropolitan Opera, Die Walküre in 1885; Opposite: cast page from the program for the Metropolitan Opera's initial performance of Die Walküre, 1885

sorrow only love may be." But already by this time, the failure of the revolution, together with Wagner's exile and broken marriage, were combining to engender a more pessimistic world view, which he then found formulated almost to perfection in Arthur Schopenhauer's *The World as Will and Representation*.

According to Schopenhauer, human desires are intrinsically evil, and the will to live is reprehensible; life is but a round of inescapable suffering, and affection or goodness to others serves only temporarily to alleviate that essential condition. As an explicit affirmation of the will to live, sexual activity should be shunned. Love in the sense of *eros* is selfish and destructive, but *agape* is acceptable, since that is tantamount to compassion or fellow suffering. Much of this Buddhist-inspired thinking Wagner was ready to accept, and it formed the philosophical basis of the newly revised ending he prepared in 1856 for *Siegfrieds Tod*, renamed *Götterdämmerung* in that year. He was reluctant, however, to go along with Schopenhauer in his rejection of *eros*, and an entry in the Venice diary of December 1858 shows him valiantly struggling to reconcile his Feuerbachian heart with his Schopenhauerian mind: "It is a question, you see, of indicating a path to salvation recognized by no philosopher, not even by Sch.[openhauer] himself, involving a total pacification of the will through love, by which I mean not some abstract love of humanity but the love which is engendered genuinely on the basis of sexual love, i.e., the attraction between man and woman." The intriguing notion of a man and woman copulating their way to salvation would have cut little ice with Schopenhauer, but Wagner was prepared to be as eclectic with his philosophies as with his medieval sources.

Love, then, might be "utterly and completely devastating," as he told his friend Röckel in 1856, but it was still a necessary part of the painful process of self-enlightenment. Love was inseparable from suffering, but suffering opened one's eyes to the delusions and self-deceptions of a world that sought meaning solely through desire. The 1856 "Schopenhauer ending" for *Götterdämmerung* was not the one finally used by Wagner, but he dropped these lines only because he felt their sense to be better conveyed by music alone, not because he rejected their sentiments. The state reached by Brünnhilde, at the end of the tetralogy as we now know it, is precisely that described by Schopenhauer in *The World as Will and Representation* as obtaining when the individual has renounced finally and fully the will to live — "an unshakable peace, a deep calm and inward serenity." It is expressed most poignantly by the orchestra immediately before the final conflagration begins, at Brünnhilde's words "Rest, rest, O god!"

This quintessentially Schopenhauerian–Buddhist moment, then, is the keynote of *Götterdämmerung*, as completed by the composer in 1874, and with it we have traced the evolution of Wagner's world view as expressed through the *Ring*, over the quarter century of its composition. It is Brünnhilde who ultimately brings peace to the gods — and, by implication, to all humanity — whereas in the original 1848 scenario it was Siegfried who was led to Valhalla, by Brünnhilde, to restore the harmonious rule of Wotan and the gods. In the course of *Siegfried* and *Götterdämmerung*, Siegfried has proved himself unworthy of the role of redeemer: in spite of his positive qualities, he simply lacks the requisite moral stature. So the succession passes from Wotan to Siegfried to Brünnhilde, and it is this last, as the representative of the *Ewig-Weibliche*, the Eternal Feminine, who brings some hope of a better future for the human race.

This need not surprise us. Life-enhancing virtues and natural forces generally are embodied by female characters in the *Ring*—ancestral wisdom by Erda and the Norns, eternal youth by Freia, innocent delight by the Rhinemaidens. The world of power politics, on the other hand, of evil, ambition, selfishness and greed, on the whole is associated with male characters. Wagner makes it clear that he holds naked male ambition responsible for the world's troubles. Only by exposing themselves to the healing, redemptive influence of woman can men hope to learn how to live. Alluding to the events in Act III of *Siegfried*, Wagner made the point to

PROGRAMME

OF THE

THIRTY-THIRD NIGHT OF THE SUBSCRIPTION.

Friday Evening, Jan. 30,

With New Scenery, Costumes, Armors and Appointments:

DIE WALKÜRE

MUSIC-DRAMA IN THREE ACTS,
BY RICHARD WAGNER.

BRUNHILDE	FRAU AMALIA MATERNA
FRICKA	FRL. MARIANNA BRANDT
SIEGLINDE	FRAU AUGUSTE KRAUS
SIEGMUND	HERR ANTON SCHOTT
WOTAN	HERR JOSEF STAUDIGL
HUNDING	HERR JOSEF KOEGEL
GERHILDE	FRL. BRANDT
ORTLINDE	FRL. STERN
WALTRAUTE	FRL. CUTJAR
SCHWERTLEITE	Walkuren. FRL. MORSE
HELMWIGE	FRAU ROBINSON
SIEGRUNE	FRL. SLACH
GRIMGERDE	FRAU KEMLITZ
ROSSWEISSE	FRL. BRANDL

Special Notice.—The preparation of the scene for the 2d
and the 3d Act, will require longer *entreacts* than usual—from
twenty-five to thirty minutes. The commencement of each act
will be signaled at the proper time by the bells in the lobbies.

The stage settings, by Herr William Hock, are after the ori-
ginal at Bayreuth.
Scenery by Messrs. Schaffer and Maeder.
Machinery arranged by Mr. A. Dornbrach.
Light effects by Mr. James Stewart, Jr.
Costumes by Mr. Dazian.
Appointments by Mr. Bradwell.
Armor and Accessories made by F. Goersch, in Berlin, who sup-
plied the composer for the first performance at Bayreuth.

Musical Director and Conductor,   -   **Dr. LEOPOLD DAMROSCH**

Stage Manager...........................Herr WILHELM HOCK
Chorus Masters.....................Herren LUND and REICHELT

**The Knabe Pianos used at the Metropolitan Opera House
and by the Artists of the Company.**

Mason & Hamlin Organs Used.

MASTER MACHINIST	A. DORNBRACH
CHIEF ENGINEER	A. S. McKAY
GAS ENGINEER	JAMES STEWART, Jr
WARDROBE MISTRESS AND COSTUME DEPARTMENT	Miss BERG
SCENIC ARTIST	Mr. SCHAEFER
PROPERTY MASTER AND ARMORER	Mr. BRADWELL
ASSISTANT STAGE MANAGER	RICHARD ZIEMIETZKI
PERRUQUIER	CHARLES MEYER
COSTUMER	Herr RITTEROTH
MUSIC LIBRARIAN	Mr. RUSSEL
ORCHESTRA MANAGER	Mr. KAYSER
DIRECTOR OF STAGE BAND	Mr. LEDERHAUS
PROMPTER	Mrs. BUSCHMANN
ADVERTISING AGENT	WILLIAM J. BROWN

The Ladies' and Gents' Coat Rooms in the Opera House are under the super-
vision of H. E. Zinn.

FLORIST........S. HOFHEIMER......ORDERS TAKEN IN THE LOBBY

TO THE PUBLIC.

The only correct and authorized edition of the Text Books, is
published by Ch. D. Koppel & Co., and sold at the principal
Music Stores, Miller's Theatre Ticket Office, 104 Broadway, and in the lobby of the Metropolitan Opera House.

All the music performed at this house can be had at G. Schirmer's
35 Union Square, New York.

King Ludwig II of Bavaria—an ardent Wagnerite, who in 1864, at age eighteen, offered the composer his patronage, making possible the completion of Der Ring des Nibelungen *as well as the building of the Festival Theater at Bayreuth—in a portrait by Friedrich Dürck, painted the year the monarch befriended Wagner*

Röckel in a letter of August 1851: "We shall not become what we can and must be until such time as—womankind has been awakened." Many similar comments of the period bear witness to Wagner's conviction that women, because intuitively sympathetic and understanding, are innately superior to men.

In this respect, at least, he remained faithful to his earlier conviction, though this is a somewhat crude generalization as regards the *Ring*. Wagner's characterization is too subtle to suggest a simple equation of female to good and male to evil. The ideal, as revealed over the course of the tetralogy, is a combination of male and female characteristics: each sex has something to offer the other. "The true human being is both man and woman," Wagner told Röckel. "Not even Siegfried alone (man alone) is the complete 'human being'; he is merely the half. Only with Brünnhilde does he become the redeemer." In our own time that proposition is rapidly making headway, but even in this post-Jungian era, it has by no means yet won universal acceptance.

Women in the *Ring* are in closer touch with the earth, its mysteries and riches. The Rhinegold, in its pure, unsullied state on the riverbed, is entrusted to the Rhinemaidens, and it is man's greed that causes this natural resource to be turned into a product that confers power, wealth and status. The ensuing catastrophe cannot be averted, but the return of the gold to its natural state is the first condition of any process of renewal.

The final conflagration is, of course, on one level, a representation of the end of the world. That such a catastrophe is brought about by man's lust for power, his abuse of the earth's natural resources, must strike us today with redoubled force. In the latter part of the twentieth century, not only have we polluted the air and waters and ravaged the forests but we have seized the secrets of the natural world to fashion weapons capable of exterminating life on the planet. If the *Ring* has one message above all for us today, it is surely that our abuse of nature, our murderously aggressive instincts and our failure to develop the full potential of our personalities—to allow our better instincts sovereignty over our lives—have set us on a course of irrevocable destruction. We have it within us to change that course. If we do not do so, we do not deserve to survive as a species.

Barry Millington is the author of the highly acclaimed Vintage Master Musicians volume Wagner, *which one reviewer described as "an account of the composer's life and career which is as close to the truth as we are currently able to get." With Stewart Spencer he is co-editor of the recently published* Selected Letters of Richard Wagner.

LEITMOTIF AND MEANING

by Carolyn Abbate

Entrance to Wagner's Festival Theater at Bayreuth, in 1876 site of the world premieres of Siegfried *and* Götterdämmerung *and in 1882 of* Parsifal

Between Acts II and III of *Siegfried*, the musical idiom characteristic of the earlier *Ring* cedes to another sonic world, denser and more dissonant than what we have heard before. When Wotan calls Erda for their cosmic chat, we know that the tetralogy has turned to its final, tragic phase, and that Wagner as composer commands a new security, a new confidence with more complex material. Small wonder: twelve years separate the creation of the two acts. In August 1857, Wagner left his "hero Siegfried dreaming under the trees" and interrupted work on the opera after finishing the orchestral draft of Act II. It was not until 1869 that he began again. In the intervening years, he wrote *Tristan und Isolde* (1857-59), the Paris revisions to *Tannhäuser* (1860-61) and *Die Meistersinger* (1862-67). The compositional experiences of these years, the radical harmonic language of *Tristan*, the rediscovery of controlled, formal patterns in *Die Meistersinger*, made possible the *Götterdämmerung* we know.

Wagner's inability to complete *Siegfried* in 1857 is one of the classic enigmas of his creative biography. Something had gone awry. We see the traces of this rupture in certain passages of Acts I and II that are, musically, some of the weakest in the *Ring*. To explain the enigma in straight aesthetic terms—that Wagner sensed he was stale, and turned to a new project as counterirritant—seems inadequate. For one thing, we know that musical ideas for *Tristan* crept upon him even as he attempted to resist them, that intrusions from *Tristan* became more and more compelling during the spring of 1857. Wagner wrote of the experience in terms of an obsession, of how *Tristan* eventually overmastered him, as if his own will had been deactivated. Why did *Tristan* compel him at just that point? His illicit passion for Mathilde Wesendonk conventionally has been cited as the inspiration for *Tristan*—an explanation which, while not ringing wholly false, seems too simple, too banal. Like all great artists, Wagner might be goaded or thwarted by external forces, but his creative evolution was shaped by its own internal concerns. Were there compositional, operatic reasons for *Tristan's* intrusive force?

Wagner's abandonment of *Siegfried* in 1857 replays, on a larger scale, an earlier event in the history of the *Ring*, the abandonment in 1850 of music for *Siegfrieds Tod* (Siegfried's Death), the original *Götterdämmerung* libretto. This text was written in 1848 and revised in 1848-50. In the summer of 1850, Wagner completed music for the Norns' scene and broke off midway through the Brünnhilde–Siegfried dialogue. (This music is nothing like what he eventually wrote in 1869 to set the analogous text in *Götterdämmerung*.) *Siegfrieds Tod* was put aside. Wagner wrote that the libretto was unsatisfactory, that too much prehistory—Siegfried's past, Brünnhilde's past, the magic Ring—had to be conveyed in long narrative passages. This dissatisfaction with narrative led him to conceive of a prefacing opera, *Der Junge Siegfried* (Young Siegfried), the story of the hero's youth. The same dissatisfaction led him in 1852 to create two further librettos dealing with Brünnhilde, Siegfried's parents and Alberich's Ring. While the *Ring* music was written over more than twenty years, from 1853 to 1874, starting with *Das Rheingold* and ending with *Götterdämmerung*, the text evolved backwards, from *Siegfrieds Tod* to *Der Junge Siegfried* to *Die Walküre* (June 1852) and *Das Rheingold* (November 1852). The complete poem finally was published in 1853, but Wagner continued to change it, often radically, in subsequent years.

The terms in which Wagner described his need to abandon the *Siegfrieds Tod* music in 1850 are similar to his later description of how *Siegfried* Act II yielded to *Tristan*. These two historical moments mark his confrontations with a musico-dramatic concept central to the *Ring*—the notion of the leitmotif. This is the device most readily identified with Wagner in the popular imagination. He is often said to have invented it, to have been the first opera composer to conceive of associating a musical gesture with some specific image, character or object, and to exploit the possibilities of the discovery. Like all historical generalizations, this one will not survive close scrutiny. Wagner was nonetheless the first to work out systematically the potential of the leitmotif, and in 1850 he was just beginning to envisage an opera woven wholly out of such motifs, without traditional numbers, without pedigreed operatic forms. In 1857 he came full circle, rejecting the leitmotif as he had first imagined it. So the two historical crises reflect a creative process that bears directly on the *Ring*.

The Bayreuth Festival Theater's "invisible" orchestra pit—the "mystic gulf"—designed to keep the stage the focus of attention as well as to blend the sonorities of Wagner's frequently heavy instrumentation with the voices of the artists charged with enacting the drama

The *Ring* notoriously establishes hundreds of musical motifs and associates them with particular poetic lines (such as Alberich's curse on the Ring), images (Valhalla) or objects (the Tarnhelm, Wotan's spear). Debussy disdainfully referred to them as orchestral "calling cards," recurring with absurd predictability to announce each character, word or prop at each appearance. Debussy's view is both cynical and simplistic. Yet his mockery of leitmotif, while it may have sprung from obsessive jealousy of Wagner, does serve to summarize straightforward instances of leitmotif in the *Ring*. Wagnerian operagoers are familiar with a motivic idea usually labeled "Sword," a trumpet fanfare adumbrated at the end of *Das Rheingold*, which winds through Act I of *Die Walküre* to emerge *fortissimo* as Siegmund pulls the sword from the tree. This motif recurs in response both to the appearance of the sword as prop and to the word *Schwert*. Predictable, repetitive, a clear sign for the object: this is a leitmotif as the term is usually understood, as Debussy understood it. But Wagner's was a more devious imagination, and the historical crises of *Siegfrieds Tod* and *Siegfried*, Act II, may nudge us toward appreciating leitmotif in more complicated ways.

Both *Siegfrieds Tod* and *Götterdämmerung* begin with a scene for the three Norns, the fates who see past, present and future, weaving their visions into a continuous rope of time. In both versions of the text, the Norns for the most part recount events that precede the tragedy about to be played. In *Siegfrieds Tod* they tell how Alberich stole the gold, how the giants bartered for Valhalla, how Siegfried killed Fafner the dragon. In *Götterdämmerung* the stories, though not the same ones, are equally concerned with the past.

This, however, is the critical difference: when the Norns in *Götterdämmerung* narrate the past, they call upon a past musical world as well, a musical world established in *Das Rheingold*, *Die Walküre*, *Siegfried*. Loge's trickery, the giants and Valhalla, Alberich, the Ring, Brünnhilde's fire—all have been enacted *to music*. These are events with a musical presence, associated with particular motifs. When the *Götterdämmerung* Norns recall events, the motifs are recalled as well, musically transformed to create a magical effect: that we hear music "out of the past." Back in 1850, however, there was only one opera: *Siegfrieds Tod* was to stand alone. Here the Norns have no musical past they can invoke, no leitmotivic hoard stored up in three previous operas. They are the beginning. Wagner's discarded music gives us Norns who sing of giants, Alberich, the Ring, not in motifs that have accumulated meaning over three previous nights, but to chords and arpeggios that are neutral, without significance.

Wagner's conception of a leitmotivic system was inspired by his dissatisfaction with the *Siegfrieds Tod* music. As he struggled to set the retrospective text he had written for the Norns, then for Siegfried and Brünnhilde, he realized that the elaborate dramatic events now only narrated must first be acted out. Their enactment would take place in music, creating a primary collection of musical symbols. The genius of the *Ring* lies in the way these symbols can later be recalled, musically transformed, when the *Ring*'s characters turn increasingly backward, looking into their world's past as that world draws to an end. In this conception the leitmotif is no mere calling card but a bearer of memories, whose transformations reflect the passage of epochal time.

Auditorium of the acoustically ideal Bayreuth Festival Theater, with its unadorned rows of wooden seats, as uncomfortable today as when Der Ring des Nibelungen *was introduced*

How can we best understand the motivic and musical eddies in Wagner's *Ring*? Wagner himself once described the cycle as a "symphonic web"—musical themes spun into ever varied patterns and forms. The implications of his phrase are well worth exploring. "Symphonic" evokes an idea of leitmotif first and foremost as purely musical matter, which can be manipulated and developed like themes in a symphony. Most of the *Ring*'s leitmotifs play a double role. They can be manipulated as symbols, standing for Valhalla, Loge, the Tarnhelm, the dragon, fate and all the rest. But their associations may broaden out, become richer over time. The motifs finally may be set free of extramusical association, combined into musical patterns.

One instance can be drawn from the very opening of the cycle. In the first scene of *Das Rheingold*, the two foolish sisters Woglinde and Wellgunde ignore cautious Flosshilde's advice and reveal to Alberich two of the Rhinegold's secrets: he who forges a ring from the gold will inherit the world, but only one who renounces love can make such a ring. Both secrets are sung to motifs that become central musical ideas in the *Ring*. An ascending-descending chain of thirds usually labeled the Ring motif underscores the first. For the second, Wagner makes certain we pay heed to Woglinde: for her words, the tempo slows, rhythm shifts to a grave, four-beat meter and a tonal environment around E major falls into C minor:

RENUNCIATION   RING

Nur wer der Min - ne Macht ent - sagt,   Reif zu zwin - gen das Gold

The melody Woglinde sings is traditionally called the renunciation motif, since it first appears in association with her ominous words. The first recurrences of this theme, moments later, as Alberich first thinks of stealing the gold, clearly are an orchestral reminder of Woglinde's warning. Alberich's climactic shout of renunciation as he seizes the gold is also sung to this motif. So far, the link between the musical gesture and renunciation of love is straightforward, as is Wagner's deliberate use of the motif in its role as *symbol*.

Later recurrences of the motif, however, suggest that both the original association with renunciation, and the very notion that the motif invariably and inevita-

bly means something, are dubious propositions. At the end of Act I of *Die Walküre*, in a gesture whose allegorical significance is as robust as it is unmistakable, Siegmund draws the sword Nothung from Hunding's oak tree, calling upon the power of love to strengthen his arm: "Heiligster Minne höchste Not." But the lines are sung to Woglinde's C-minor motif. What has renunciation of love to do with Siegmund's words or deed? The *putative* meaning of the motif seems at war with Siegmund's text, for, far from renouncing love, Siegmund here embraces it fully.

A similar apparent contradiction appears in Act I of *Götterdämmerung* when Brünnhilde, asked by Waltraute to return the accursed Ring to the Rhinemaidens, refuses. The Ring, she says, is Siegfried's pledge to her, the avatar of their love. To give it away would be to make a symbolic gesture rejecting that love, and Brünnhilde "would never abandon love":

die Lie - be lies - se ich nie

Here, renouncing love is not an option.

In both instances, however, it is not Wagner who is somehow at fault or inconsistent. *We* have caused the schism. If we are trapped in an uncompromising notion that a leitmotif is a calling card, that the motif represents some fixed image, then we are forced to postulate contradictions between the motif's supposed meaning and the way it is used in these examples.

This is not to say that Woglinde's motif is without associations—only that they are more complex than we allow, accessible only if we go beyond the calling card. The motif in its original C-minor form recurs at solemn, ceremonial moments: Woglinde, Alberich, Siegmund and Brünnhilde are alike in using it to make formal statements that will produce profound moral consequences for the *Ring*. In this symbolic nexus, the motif does not signify any particular image or idea but instead marks critical ritual declarations. The C-minor key, slow tempo, four-beat thump, simple melodic arch: these are the musical means that lend the theme its gravity, darkly underscoring the words it sets.

Prominent Ring artists at the Metropolitan Opera 1885-1900: Above: Amalie Materna as Brünnhilde; Top row, opposite page: Joseph Beck as Alberich, Emil Fischer as Wotan, Lilli Lehmann as Brünnhilde, Albert Niemann as Siegmund; Second row: Sophie Traubmann as Woglinde, Max Alvary as Siegfried, Jean De Reszke as Siegfried, David Bispham as Alberich; Third row: Emma Eames as Sieglinde, Lillian Nordica as Brünnhilde, Edouard De Reszke as Hagen, Ernestine Schumann-Heink as Waltraute; Bottom row: Ernest Van Dyck as Loge, Anton Van Rooy as the Wanderer, Milka Ternina as Brünnhilde, Hans Breuer as Mime

Like all the *Ring*'s motifs, Woglinde's melody mutates into new forms. In distorted, dissonant guise it winds through Wotan's tragic realization that he must permit Siegmund's death, in the narrative monologue of *Die Walküre*, Act II:

I touched Alberich's Ring,	Ich berührte Alberichs Ring,
In greed reached for the gold!	gierig hielt ich das Gold!
The curse that I fled,	Der Fluch, den ich floh,
Now it pursues me:	nicht flieht er nun mich:
All that I love,	Was ich liebe,
I must abandon,	muss ich verlassen,
Murder whatever I cherish,	morden, wen je ich minne,
Betray treacherously	trügend verraten
All that I hold dear!	wer mir traut!

Here the motif carries its poetic meaning as a marker of hieratic declarations, as well as its original, more literal association with renunciation: Wotan speaks of abandoning, murdering and betraying the objects of his love.

Elsewhere, however, the transformed motif also is used neutrally, as compositional matter, bearing none of its associations. As one of the most frequently used cadential formulas in the *Ring*, it often crops up as a closing gesture at the end of longer musical phrases, as in this line of Hagen's from the conspiracy scene in *Götterdämmerung*, Act II:

Over the four nights of the *Ring*, what began with Woglinde and Alberich as an apparently traditional leitmotif, representing a single fixed idea, is divested of its initial association with renunciation to take on a more complicated poetic function. It metamorphoses into new forms, shedding its extramusical connotations. What happens to the renunciation motif warns us to be skeptical of accepting any of the other leitmotifs as mere calling cards. Indeed, the *Ring* includes many whose life story runs in just the opposite direction: beginning as unfixed, neutral musical matter they gradually become more defined, taking on different meanings in each new context. One of these is a four-note motif known as the flight motif, because its first extensive use is in the orchestral accompaniment to Freia's entrance in *Das Rheingold*, as she tries to escape the giants:

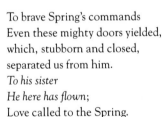

Wahnfried, Wagner's home
in Bayreuth, built in 1873, thanks
to magnanimous underwriting by King Ludwig

Many critics have argued that its meaning must go beyond, since it recurs in situations where flight is furthest from anyone's mind. But this critical wrangle only sidesteps a more radical proposition—that the motif has no extramusical meaning. For one thing, the music that accompanies Freia's entrance is little more than wallpaper, setting off her panicked voice. Repetitions pattern the paper, and we hardly note the motif as having its own identity, much less an instant symbolic force. For another, Wagner does forge intricate associations for the motif, but they differ greatly from scene to scene. The motif, then, is neutral: it can become a symbol, but its natural state is purely musical. In *Die Walküre*, Act I, it becomes poetically meaningful during Siegmund's Spring Song and its denouement. During this act the motif has recurred often, but in nebulous form, often in the solo cello during the pantomime music for Sieglinde's and Siegmund's mute exchange of glances. When not sung, it is not connected to specific words. This changes in the Spring Song, when Siegmund sings two critical text lines (here italicized) to the motif:

To brave Spring's commands	Wohl musste den tapfern Streichen
Even these mighty doors yielded,	die strenge Türe auch weichen,
which, stubborn and closed,	die trotzig und starr
separated us from him.	uns—trennte von ihm.
To his sister	Zu seiner Schwester
He here has flown;	schwang er sich her;
Love called to the Spring.	die Liebe lockte den Lenz.

The Spring Song is a story about Brother Spring and Sister Love, united in Hunding's house. The motif marks two lines that are a first clue in decoding the allegory. To be sure, the audience already knows that Siegmund and Sieglinde are brother and sister, separated long ago and reunited on this night. For the Wälsung twins themselves the revelation comes more slowly; the Spring Song sets the process in motion, and they will gradually decode the riddle it proposes. Sieglinde takes the next step in her reply to Siegmund:

Du   bist   der   Lenz

Here the motif is sung strongly—nebulous no more, independent, a declarative initial phrase. Musically, the theme is now fully realized. Beyond this, it marks Sieglinde's words "*You* are the Spring," the brother.

Within this local context, Wagner uses the motif to signal each stage in unraveling the symbolism of Brother Spring and his lost sister. He allows this melodic idea to absorb an extramusical significance, exploiting it self-consciously and precisely. Once the scene is over, this function drains from the motif, leaving it as it had been—a musical thought. Free to float without poetic associations, free to absorb meanings and discard them, the motif is one of hundreds whose workings are similar, woven into Wagner's "symphonic web."

Few would deny that the *Ring* is the most "leitmotivic" of Wagner's works, since many of its motifs are in fact used often in straight representational fashion. This becomes a powerful device: the motifs can whisper to the audience things the characters onstage cannot begin to guess. The transformation music between Scenes 1 and 2 of *Das Rheingold* provides a classic instance. The Ring motif's chain of thirds sounds over and over again in the orchestra, taking on a new harmonic color each time. As the curtain goes up on Scene 2, the motivic kaleidoscope is given a last turn, and the ascending-descending thirds of the Ring motif become the ascending-descending chords of the Valhalla motif, which sounds at the moment we *see* the fortress. By making a musical connection between the two motifs—one engenders the other—Wagner also makes a philosophical point. Wotan's power, of which Valhalla is the visible sign, is as corrupt, as undermined and precarious, as the power the Ring lends to Alberich.

Ivy-covered crypt in the gardens behind Wahnfried holding the remains of Richard and Cosima Wagner, yet another project for which the composer supervised construction

Wagner's use of leitmotif, however, changes radically at the point where he interrupted his work on the *Ring*—between Acts II and III of *Siegfried*. The simple, symbolic correspondences for the most part fade away, replaced by the more ambiguous gestures prefigured in the composer's earlier manipulation of the renunciation and flight motifs. In *Götterdämmerung* the motifs have become so rich and diffuse in their associations, so transformed in their musical habitus, that the effect is one not of a dictionary but of a symphony, whose themes have what Thomas Mann called the "magic of interrelatedness."

Wagner's suspension of the *Siegfried* project after Act II, the second crisis in the *Ring*'s gestation, can be seen, like the first, as a crisis of the leitmotif. *Tristan* began to absorb Wagner's imagination; purely musical ideas would come to him, he wrote, and he would not be certain what part of the *Tristan* poem they "belonged to," not even which act. The remark is suggestive. In *Tristan* there are no leitmotifs: with rare exceptions, its motifs are not given extramusical associations. When Wagner responded in 1857 to *Tristan*'s demands for embodiment, he was responding to a new vision of textual-musical relationships, one radically different from the leitmotivic system of the earlier parts of the *Ring*.

When he returned to *Siegfried* in 1869-71 and at last to *Götterdämmerung* in 1869-74, the experience of *Tristan* would resonate into the *Ring*'s final stages. Mann's *Beziehungszauber*, that "magical interrelatedness" we perceive in the *Ring*, was born when Wagner decided to give the Norns a hoard of symbolic motifs, created in the earlier operas, recapitulated as the cycle draws to an end. The overwhelming magic is owed not to leitmotivic symbolism—any composer can master the art of the calling card. A musical web, motivic transformation, a nexus of poetic associations that become more and more complex, music that in the final hours seems to be heard from a distant and unrecoverable past—these were Wagner's new means, the lessons of *Tristan*.

Carolyn Abbate is Assistant Professor of Music at Princeton University. Her latest book, Narrative, Opera and Music's Voice, *will be published in 1989.*

Siegfried Death

Earliest known photograph taken onstage at the Metropolitan Opera: Act III, Scene 1, of Götterdämmerung, *published in the March 1, 1890, issue of* Illustrated American, *with insets of conductor Anton Seidl, Lilli Lehmann as Brünnhilde and composer Richard Wagner. Also shown are cast pages from the programs for the company premieres of* Siegfried, *1887, and* Götterdämmerung, *1888*

 23

WAGNER AS POET

by Richard Howard

Wagner reading at his desk during the period when the text and music of Der Ring des Nibelungen *totally engaged his energies*

In a hundred years, it is generally assumed that the air clears, the dust settles, and a sharpened perspective reveals, as down a corridor of continuous revelation, the Truth about Art. Indeed, in what Nietzsche called the Case of Wagner (already the suggestion is flagrant: we are dealing with a matter somewhere between the police court and the pathology laboratory), many issues have been ventilated, if not laundered, to consensual satisfaction. As with many another sacred monster of romanticism, from Goethe to Turner (to Freud?), we feel that with all these decades to do it in, we have at last penetrated and plucked the heart out of mysteries from which the mere glamour of a Figure's presence had debarred us. After a century we think we know better: we believe we have *the goods*.

In the case of Wagner, of course, it is the bads, though it comes to much the same thing. All revelations about the creative life that are not banausic are exorcisms, whether it is the saintly Chekhov we exsufflate or the satanic Sade, or even the suburban Brahms. We know nowadays, with the easy wealth of contemporary documentation to abet our spying, our inquisition, our demystification, that Wagner was a con man and a (successful) crook; that he was a spiteful brat, a hypocritical philanderer, a jealous and infantile spoiler of his musical peers; that his tastes—it is W. H. Auden who casts the stone—in dress and decor were those of a drag queen; and more detestably still, that he was an anti-Semite of the deepest dye (whatever color that might be: he seems much closer to twentieth-century nadirs here than to his "normal" Jew-hating contemporaries) and a nationalist of the most reckless stripe, furious at Bismarck for not razing Paris when he had the chance.

After such knowledge, as the poet says, is the creative exemplification of all the bourgeois virtues of industry, tidiness, attention to detail and professional finish sufficient to gain our forgiveness? Not our forgiveness, probably, but our sufferance. For in art the combination of genius with those same virtues, as this centenary attests, triumphs over "mere" ethical considerations, though the ruins of such a victory may be eternal. Witness the nervousness of our new productions, the uncertainty as to how much of the Master's personal *Stimmung* can be allowed to permeate his presented works.

As a writer, as a poet myself, I am concerned that in all this chorus of revision and revaluation, still resounding with regard to the Wagner canon, so little is said about the verses that constitute the dorsal columns of the music dramas. I should like to loiter over the question of Wagnerian poetry, even as we must consider it in English. Fortunately my task is made possible by the existence of Andrew Porter's really good translations of the *Ring, Tristan* and *Parsifal*. Though intended to be sung, acted and heard, not "merely" read, Porter's versions present us with the same kinds of problems we face with the originals, if not inveterately with the much vexed solutions. For example, Wagner first composed his texts in prose. At the end of May 1852 he writes to his friend Uhlig, "I now have finished the complete draft of *Die Walküre*. Tomorrow I shall make a start on the verses." Less than a month elapses before he writes Liszt, "I am hard at work, hoping to finish the poem of my *Walküre* within the next two weeks. . . . It is turning out to be terribly beautiful! I hope to be able to submit the *entire* poem of the tetralogy to you before the end of the summer. The music will then proceed very easily and quickly, for it is *simply* a question of carrying out what is already *finished*."

As these quotations rather terrifyingly reveal, in Wagner's theory (and practice, through *Siegfried* at least), words are at least as important as music, and the "poem" affords the conceptual elements that beget the musician's vocal line. Yet for Wagner, neither music nor poetry is in theory important; what is important is pre-verbal drama, symbolic gesture and tableau (myth). Imagine a poet, then, compelled to create dramas in which the words must somehow erase themselves even as they do their work—in which that great Wagnerian topos *renunciation* must function primarily on the creative, the organizational level. That is, the words must give way to the music, and the music must give way to the drama, and whenever the "ideas" associated with the original words have special significance, the drama itself must give way to repetition and motivic elaboration. This is why the Wagner opera falls (rises?) into acts rather than numbers, and why the sustained thematic developments "look to" a Beethoven symphony rather than to a Gluck aria.

The title page of Wagner's manuscript for Der Ring des Nibelungen, dated 1873, with dedication to his patron and friend King Ludwig II of Bavaria

What a paradox! Here is a body of texts, obscure to a degree (even in Germany, we are told, it is fashionable to feign bewilderment and even scorn for the Wagnerian poem), which because of their musical and dramatic setting (calculated juxtapositions of rhythm, accent, pitch and key relationships) have held the stage for a century—indeed have triumphed over all other kinds of operatic writing, with regard to "influence" and musical posterity—precisely because they are not to be singled out as poetry, as memorable speech. One might say that Wagner is the most successful German poet since Goethe just because no one can remember his words (except, one trusts, the singers). Of course we must not forget that Wagner is a powerful writer, a writer of prose, for all the fuss and blunderbuss of the theoretical pamphlets: surely the self-creation of his autobiography stands with Goethe's and Canetti's, stands just halfway between them, as one of the liveliest and most formidable myths of identity ever forged in German (the right verb here, if ever there was one). But as a *poet*, Wagner's achievement requires a good deal of special treatment, if not special pleading.

In *Opera and Drama* Wagner claims that the German language does not readily accommodate traditional end-rhyme, but rather is suited to the primeval alliterative language (*Stabreim*) of that remote age when the Folk was both poet and mythmaker. Whatever the claims of theory in this regard (my favorites are advanced by one of Wagner's contemporaries named Ulrich Pretzel!), the composer-poet devised a quite personal expressive language out of the technical contraptions and expressive modes of identifiable predecessors and contemporaries. So well did he succeed that it has been claimed (by Peter Branscombe, in an astute essay, *Wagner as Poet*) that the transfer of even a few lines from one of Wagner's mature works to another is unthinkable—an assertion we can make with regard to no operatic predecessor, not even Da Ponte. And of course the Master himself was never short on admiration for his own productions, quite prepared to argue their autonomous poetic virtues: "I cannot deny myself the fancy," he wrote to his half-sister Cäcilie, who had married one of his publishers, "that this poem [*The Ring*], on its own terms, should win renown and lasting regard purely as a literary manifestation."

The world has been correct not to go along with Wagner here, for he was allowing his habitual vanity to defeat his actual and authentic achievement. Of course there are moments, situations, when the words are memorable. Usually they are comic moments, for as Gide (an unpersuadable Wagner-hater, and therefore an interesting witness for the defense) observed in his journal in 1907, Wagner, like Hugo, always excels in moments of comic truculence: has there ever been a performance of *Siegfried* when the audience fails to laugh at the hero's inevitable discovery that the sleeping Brünnhilde is "no man"? Or of *Götterdämmerung* when Gunther, with comparable ingenuousness, seeing Hagen thrust his spear into Siegfried's back, inquires, "Hagen, what are you doing?" But I should like to elicit a more serious instance, a more telling one. Let us revert to my favorite scene in the whole tetralogy, a scene quite comparable to Antigone's claims to Creon of a "higher law"—the opening of the final scene of *Die Walküre*. Her sisters have left Brünnhilde alone at her father's feet, and after a long silence, beginning timidly and becoming more confident, his favorite daughter asks Wotan:

Prominent Ring *artists at the Metropolitan Opera 1900-17: Above: Jacques Urlus as Siegmund; Top row, opposite page: Albert Reiss as Mime, Luise Reuss-Belce as Fricka, Alois Burgstaller as Siegfried, Olive Fremstad as Sieglinde; Second row: Johanna Gadski as Brünnhilde, Otto Goritz as Alberich, Louise Homer as Fricka, Allen Hinckley as Hunding; Third row: Margarete Matzenauer as Brünnhilde, Hermann Weil as Wotan, Putnam Griswold as Hagen, Basil Millspaugh Ruysdael as Donner; Bottom row: Carl Jörn as Loge, Melanie Kurt as Brünnhilde, Johannes Sembach as Siegfried, Marie Rappold as Freia*

War es so schmählich,	Was it so shameful,
was ich verbrach,	what I have done,
dass mein Verbrechen so	that you must punish my
schmählich du strafst?	deed with endless shame?
War es so niedrig,	Was it disgraceful
was ich dir tat,	what I have done;
dass du so tief mir	do I deserve to be
Erniedrigung schaffst?	plunged in disgrace?
War es so ehrlos,	Was my dishonor
was ich beging,	boundless and base,
dass mein Vergeh'n nun	for that offense must
die Ehre mir raubt?	my honor be lost?
O sag, Vater!	Oh speak, father!
Sieh mir ins Auge:	Look in my eyes:
schweige den Zorn,	silence your scorn,
zähme die Wut	soften your wrath,
und deute mir hell	explain to me
die dunkle Schuld,	all the grievous guilt
die mit starrem	that compels you,
Trotze dich zwingt	cruel and harsh,
zu verstossen dein	to abandon your true,
trautestes Kind!	loving child.

If not Sophoclean, at least the text has that unmistakable twist of idiom, that diction of necessity we call Shakespearean, meaning a sort of shorthand for *eloquent, resourceful and unexpected*, as when Caliban says "I must eat my dinner." Nor would I dare suggest that these moments when Wagner's poetry transcends its obligatory oblivion are not precisely moments when the Master himself was committed to a psychodrama of his own, one that could not be transcended in more intimate terms. Each of us will have his choices of these successes (failures, in terms of what the musical text demands); the fact that our selections will vary is perhaps a stronger argument for Wagner's gift as a dramatic poet, *tout court*, than I had assumed. Moreover, on the evidence I have collected from my friends who watched the Boulez telecasts from Bayreuth, even those of us who supposed we had a pretty sure grasp of the verbal particulars in the tetralogy were astonished by the enhancement our response to the *dramas* received from that little ribbon of text glittering beneath the images on the screen: who knows the words so well, we found, that a textual refreshment is out of order?

Marble bust of Richard Wagner by the sculptor Arno Breker, now positioned in the rose garden near the entrance of the Bayreuth Festival Theater

What must be memorable in the text must be memorable, as I have suggested, chiefly for the singers. And as a set of mnemonic signals, the Wagner poems are invincible. Let me leave this part of the argument, though I intend nothing so polemic as an argument, with the suggestion, then, that the texts of the Wagner operas are so many runes, magic devices whereby the meaning can be furthered without the necessity of poetry as the spoken theater has understood "poetry." Eliot is perhaps the first modern poet to invoke Wagner's *runic* use, as his quotations from *Tristan* and the *Ring* in *The Waste Land* attest. And a further comparison seems to me the likeliest way of accounting for the success, as I hear it, of Wagner's lines of verse: consider the screenplays of those Hollywood films of the thirties and forties which we remember of course chiefly as the vehicles for Davis, for Hepburn, for Crawford. The words uttered (uttered! were they not sung, crooned, howled, intoned as fatefully as any *Heldensopran*'s performance?) have little merit as specimens of dramatic diction; we patronize the screenplays of *Now, Voyager* or *A Woman's Face* just as we condescend to the verses of *Das Rheingold*, yet I contend the latter possess an analogous and effective charm, the same runic power: through them the drama runs, as in an irrigation trench, and the power of Wagner's poetry, analogous to the businesslike dialogue of *Possessed* or *Dark Victory*, is that it never (never? rarely, as rarely as it transcends itself into memorable poetry) obstructs the movement of the drama, the symbolic *gestus*, the myth. It is a reluctant poetry we shall be afforded, perhaps, by the Wagner operas, but it is a real poetry nonetheless, and if we cannot, as with Dante to Virgil, say "Honor to the highest poet," we can—and I believe we must—say "Honor to the poet who most renounces poetry." The honor we pay is to listen, of course, as we do, as we shall do.

Richard Howard's ninth book of poetry, No Traveller, *will be published next March by Knopf. A translator and critic as well, he is the Ropes Professor of Comparative Literature at the University of Cincinnati.*

GODS, DEMIGODS AND MORTALS

by Benjamin Ivry

BRÜNNHILDE

Valkyrie, favorite child of Wotan by Erda, thorn in Fricka's side. With a helmet, breastplate and spear to manipulate, Brünnhilde is an extremely challenging role, even for a goddess of a singing actress. Daughter, sister, warrior maiden, lover, bride, wronged wife, widow and finally suicide, in *Die Walküre* she is a rebel, sentenced by her angry father to sleep on a rock. In *Siegfried* she is awakened from a two-decade nap, as expected, by the innocent young hero Siegfried, her half nephew. An involved, often confusing, duet follows, during which Brünnhilde expresses anxiety about losing her virginity, her immortality—already lost—and all else that love makes her renounce. Couples rarely live happily ever after in Wagner's world, but *Siegfried* does end joyfully. In *Götterdämmerung* Brünnhilde plays her greatest part—the redeemer of mankind through her sacrifice.

SIEGMUND

Mortal son of Wotan, a Wälsung, lover of Sieglinde, his twin, father of the hero Siegfried. Wotan has raised Siegmund, hoping the youth will be able to defeat the giant/dragon Fafner and regain the Ring for the gods. Unfortunately, as his stepmother, Fricka, points out, Siegmund cannot fulfill this wish, for three reasons. First, he has committed adultery with Hunding's wife, Sieglinde. Second, Sieglinde is his sister, so both are guilty of incest. Third, Siegmund is related to Wotan and therefore cannot fill the role of a redeemer who has no connection to the god. Siegmund therefore must be killed in his duel with Hunding. At one point he tells Brünnhilde he would rather stay in hell with Sieglinde than spend eternity in Paradise without her. His words convince Brünnhilde she must shield him in defiance of her father's will. In the end, Siegmund, whatever his sins, is far more admirable than Wagner's full-fledged deities.

SIEGLINDE

Hunding's wife, Wotan's mortal daughter, a Wälsung, Siegmund's sister and lover, mother of Siegfried. This role offers rich contrasts, ranging from ecstatic love to immense grief. Because of their sympathetic plight, she and Siegmund persuade the audience to overlook any scruples about an incestuous relationship. After Siegmund dies, Sieglinde is self-possessed enough to flee with her half sister Brünnhilde and to preserve the fragments of the sword, given her by the Valkyrie. Although newly widowed and undone by her loss, when Brünnhilde tells her she will bear Siegmund's child, Sieglinde stoically accepts her fate and retreats alone to the wilderness to await delivery.

Sieglinde in Die Walküre, costume design by Rolf Langenfass for the Metropolitan Opera's new production of Wagner's music drama, 1986

SIEGFRIED

Son of Sieglinde and Siegmund, grandson of Wotan and therefore half nephew of his beloved, Brünnhilde, and despite his own objections, foster son of Mime. Innocent and noble, Siegfried is the hero without fear. His brushes with nature include capture of a bear. He also has the luck to understand the Forest Bird's pocket explanation of the *Ring*'s plot, not by virtue of any profound identification with nature, but because he accidentally has tasted dragon's blood. Born an iconoclast, ready to sweep away the old order, Siegfried derives his strength partially from ignorance. One of his most constant traits is impatience with elders, Mime and Wotan both reaping the youth's scorn.

WOTAN

Wotan in Die Walküre *as painted by designer Rolf Langenfass for the 1986 production of Wagner's music drama at the Metropolitan Opera*

Leader of the gods. This does not mean, however, that he has a perfect character, so don't let a noble manner and resonant voice delude you. In fact, Wotan has as many personality problems as Richard Wagner himself. Like Wagner, Wotan is aware of his failings and examines each one minutely during the course of *Der Ring des Nibelungen*. In *Das Rheingold* we learn that he has accepted the advice of Loge on how to con Fasolt and Fafner into building Valhalla. Wotan is not the first customer to try to cheat an architect, but the lengths he goes to in trying to evade his obligations are unique. On the domestic front, Wotan is chronically unfaithful to his wife, Fricka. In love and war, building and destruction, Wotan cuts an imposing figure. For all his faults, his lengthy, agonized soul-searching makes him one of the most tragic figures of the entire cycle. One senses his presence, even in *Götterdämmerung*—sitting in Valhalla, waiting for the end.

FRICKA

Wotan's legal wife, sister to Freia, Froh and Donner. Like the rest of the gods, Fricka has her flaws. She has encouraged Wotan to build Valhalla, cause of the gods' travails. Part of her motive is to keep Wotan from his countless philanderings (see "Erda," below). Fricka fits nicely into the tradition of the deceived operatic spouse. The special irony here, of course, is that Fricka is the deity of marriage. Some may find her condemnation of Siegmund and Sieglinde too rigid and unfeeling, but she is merely fulfilling her responsibilities, and don't forget that Siegmund and Sieglinde are Wotan's illegitimate offspring. Given her strong character, a revaluation of Fricka seems overdue. Often she is compared to Wagner's first wife, Minna. Critics sometimes label as "marital bickering" the scene between Fricka and her husband. In fact, it is among the most telling in all the *Ring*.

LOGE

The demigod of fire, a trickster who serves as counselor to Wotan. Related to both the Nibelungs and the gods, he calls Alberich cousin. This mischief-maker hatches schemes too devious for the other gods. In Loge, writers and performing artists may see similarities to the careerists known as agents. Loge conceives the plan to bilk the giants of their fee for building Valhalla and connives in the capture of Alberich's all-powerful Ring. At underhanded tactics, Wotan is no match for his adviser.

FREIA

Goddess of youth, also known as Holda, who tends the golden apples that are essential for the gods' continual rejuvenation. As a singing role, Freia seems rather one-dimensional: for the most part she only rushes about trying to avoid the giants and imploring help. But Freia is not merely a passive pawn in the action of the *Ring*. In *Die Walküre*, though she does not herself appear, as goddess of love she instigates the union of Sieglinde and Siegmund. When Sieglinde tells her brother-lover "You are the spring," she is technically wrong: Freia is the spring. But Wagner's characters are never as fussy about mythography as Wagner's critics are.

FROH AND DONNER

Brothers of Fricka and Freia. Froh, a bright, likable character, creates the rainbow in the final scene of *Das Rheingold*, providing the gods a colorful path to Valhalla. By contrast, Donner, god of thunder, is rather bellicose by nature. Both characters make their strongest impression when the giants Fafner and Fasolt enter to demand Freia as payment for Valhalla. They swell the varied assembly of giants, gnomes and normal-sized gods. Froh's charming arietta "Wie liebliche Luft" celebrates his sister's (and youth's) return. This melody is one of the few truly hummable tunes in the entire tetralogy.

ERDA

Earth Mother, all-knowing goddess who gives birth to the Norns and the Valkyries. In *Das Rheingold* Erda materializes from the earth, warning Wotan to surrender the Ring to Fasolt and Fafner. Sometime between this event and those of *Die Walküre*, Wotan has courted Erda, engendering nine warrior daughters. In *Siegfried* Wotan again visits his old flame to learn if the course of destiny can be altered. Erda is sluggish, however, and suggests that Wotan ask the Norns or Brünnhilde instead. The latter is still asleep on her rock, and Erda dozes off too, as inert as a Beckett heroine.

FASOLT AND FAFNER

A pair of earthling brothers, giants, among the more sympathetic characters in the *Der Ring des Nibelungen*. Their first entrance is announced by thumping percussion, somewhat reminiscent of the stomp of the Commendatore's statue in Mozart's *Don Giovanni*. In *Das Rheingold*, driven by lust for the Ring, Fafner commits fratricide. By the time of *Die Walküre* he has transformed himself into a frightful dragon, but he does not appear in monster guise until *Siegfried*, when the youthful hero confronts him. Fafner, who hibernates in a cave, guarding his gold, seems stupefied by Siegfried's attack. He succumbs instantly, with the vague regret that he has not heard of his slayer.

ALBERICH AND MIME

Another pair of brothers, in this case gnomes of the Nibelung tribe, miners and tinkers who live in caves. Alberich, who sneezes underwater, and who by his theft of the Rhinegold precipitates the plot of *Der Ring des Nibelungen*, should not be pitied for the abuse he receives. Wagner felt he deserved every bit of his torment. The hatred he engenders is as much instinctual as rational. Though an audience might be inclined to sympathize with Mime, forger of the Ring and the magic Tarnhelm, also the butt of much abuse, Siegfried's taunts are merely examples of hearty Wagnerian humor. As if this character were not hapless enough, George Bernard Shaw added further insult by initiating a "spelling reform" in *The Perfect Wagnerite*. In this study, Mime's name is spelled "Mimmy." The scene in which his thoughts are revealed to Siegfried, who can divine his hypocrisy, seems like an odd prefiguration of O'Neill's *Strange Interlude*.

HUNDING

Sieglinde's husband and partially, at least, an admirable character. True, by marrying Sieglinde, who does not love him, Hunding offends the romantic ideal. But to his credit, when a stranger bursts into his home Hunding obeys the laws of hospitality: Siegmund may spend the night before facing his host in combat the following morning. The guest takes advantage of this reprieve to sing a love duet with Hunding's wife, who has drugged her spouse. Modern audiences may feel sympathy for this cuckolded figure, but such was scarcely Wagner's intent. The composer surely felt this marital stick-in-the-mud gets his just deserts when Wotan puts him to death with a single glance.

Erda in Das Rheingold *as designed by Rolf Langenfass for the Metropolitan Opera's 1987 production of the prologue to* Wagner's Der Ring des Nibelungen

Gunther in Götterdämmerung as depicted by costume designer Rolf Langenfass for the Metropolitan Opera's 1988 staging of this music drama

Das Rheingold, as staged in the new production at the Metropolitan Opera: Opposite, Scene 4: Wotan, leader of the gods (James Morris), exults after plundering the Ring from the Nibelung gnome Alberich; Overleaf one, Scene 1: under the waters of the river, the Rhinemaidens—Wellgunde (Diane Kesling), Flosshilde (Meredith Parsons) and Woglinde (Mi Hae Park)— guard their golden treasure; Overleaf two, Scene 2: as Valhalla towers above them in the distance, Donner (Philip Joll), Fafner (Aage Haugland), Fasolt (John Macurdy) and Wotan (James Morris) witness the arrival of Loge (Siegfried Jerusalem), after which the fire god describes Alberich's omnipotent Ring to Fricka (Waltraud Meier), Donner (Philip Joll), the other gods and the giants

FOREST BIRD

Species unspecified. This offstage voice enchants the hero—and the public—during the Forest Murmurs scene of *Siegfried*. At first we hear merely birdsong, but after tasting the blood of the dragon, Siegfried is able to understand his feathered friend—and so does the audience. This turns out to be essential to the plot: the bird reveals the whereabouts of the Ring and the Tarnhelm. Because the part is tiny but integral to the story, it has often taken flight with famous sopranos.

GIBICHUNGS

Gunther, Gutrune and Hagen appear only in *Götterdämmerung*. The mother of this unsavory family, Grimhild, gave birth first to Gunther and Gutrune, who are the rulers of the Gibichung clan; their father was Gibich. Hagen, their younger half brother, was born to Grimhild after her liaison with Alberich, which the gnome has paid for with gold. So much for Grimhild's reputation. Gutrune develops an instant crush on Siegfried but realizes she hasn't a prayer of winning him without a love potion. Gunther conspires to use Siegfried so he can marry Brünnhilde, whom he comes to idolize, though she does not return his admiration. The ex-Valkyrie chides Gunther, "Deeply has your glorious race sunk, to bear a coward like you." Despite heavy-handed joking with the tribesmen, Hagen takes the initiative in villainy. After Siegfried is slain, the Ring is reclaimed from his finger by Brünnhilde. Hagen drowns in his attempt to take it: before he dies, he utters the final words of the drama, "Zurück vom Ring!" (Get back from the Ring!).

RHINEMAIDENS

Mermaids. Woglinde, Wellgunde and Flosshilde are custodians of the Rhinegold but relinquish their treasure fairly easily to Alberich at the beginning of the *Ring*. They also banter with Siegfried in *Götterdämmerung*, though they then make the error of trying to scare the hero into returning the Ring. He is incapable of fear and resists the nymphs completely. These daughters of the river emphasize the power of destiny throughout the entire cycle. Students of the *Ring* have detected differences among Rhinemaidens (Flosshilde has been termed the "least vacuous"), but this is more than most audiences can do.

VALKYRIES

Nine daughters of Wotan and Erda. Their names are Gerhilde, Helmwige, Waltraute, Schwertleite, Ortlinde, Siegrune, Grimgerde, Rossweisse, and the most famous of their number is Brünnhilde. Memorize all of them successfully and you will triumph in barroom debates. The Valkyries, Joan of Arc-like, are warrior maidens who recruit dead heroes to guard their father's fortress, Valhalla. Besides Brünnhilde, only Waltraute plays a significant role. In *Götterdämmerung* this worried figure makes a stealthy, fruitless visit to her banished sister, begging her to return the Ring to the Rhinemaidens. She departs on a high A "Weh!"

NORNS

Three nameless fates. Their roles are pure metaphor: they embody past, present and future—the destiny of the Wagnerian universe. Their only appearance is in *Götterdämmerung*, though Erda mentions them in *Siegfried*. Erda is the mother of the Norns, so they are half sisters to the Valkyries; their paternity remains a mystery. The Norns inform us that Wotan has stacked piles of sacred wood around the walls of his fortress, Valhalla. There the leader of the gods waits for the final burst of flames that will finish his rule. The rope of destiny that the Norns weave eventually snaps, foretelling an end to four long evenings of music drama.

Benjamin Ivry is a poet and critic. His articles and reviews have appeared in many publications in the U.S.A., Great Britain and France. His latest book, Regatta, *was published by Simon and Schuster in 1988.*

DAS RHEINGOLD

RING TALES

by Faubion Bowers

Henry Fothergill Chorley, England's preeminent music critic for the *Athenaeum* journal, sojourned in Germany, where he "witnessed the production of certain musical dramas by one who has since made some noise in the world, and who is likely to make more—noise, strictly speaking—not music." Despite his negative assessment, deemed at the time to be "fair-minded," some felt otherwise. After the *Ring* was performed *in toto* at Bayreuth in 1876, a young philosopher, writer and Junker friend of Wagner's, Edmund Von Hagen, exclaimed in print, "Look up, dust-born humanity, to the sunny light! There you see Plato, you see Kant, you see Schopenhauer, those solitary geniuses of all time, all-powerful and gigantic. Yet above all these towers one genius—Richard Wagner. Hail to thee, Plato; hail to thee, Kant, and to thee hail, Schopenhauer. Hail to all of you old geniuses; but three times hail to you, Wagner."

As early as 1888 there were 244 branches and agencies of the Wagner Society worldwide, with upwards of 6,000 members and an international newspaper of their own called "The Meister." The editor of the *Bayreuther Blatter*, Hans von Wolzogen, established the shaky doctrine that "Only those who adore Wagner have the right to judge his work." In 1889 the then music critic George Bernard Shaw wrote, "Oh Bayreuth, Bayreuth, valley of humiliation for the smart ones of the world! To think that this Wagner, once the very safest man in Europe to ridicule, should turn out the prime success of the century."

Nietzsche the philosopher, once Wagner's partisan, savaged the composer in *Der Fall Wagner* (The Case of Wagner). He found the music "bad for young men and fatal to women." As for himself, he said, "I can no longer breathe with ease when the music begins." His throat became sore and had to be relieved with Gerandel's pastilles. Anguished he wrote, "Just look at all those youthlets, all benumbed, pale and breathless! They are Wagnerites: they know nothing about music—and yet Wagner gets the mastery of them."

Wagner had finished the score of *Die Walküre* by 1856, but its staging waited fourteen years for its Munich premiere. On June 26, 1870, the *Musikalisches Wochenblatt* described the disaster: "The performance was in every respect a complete failure…artists of mediocre ability…scenic effects inferior and absurd…the magic fire was produced by a few pails of burning alcohol which flowed through a groove past the stage. The crackling noise which accompanied the rising flames frightened the public to such an extent that one part of the audience started to leave, and the effect of the music was entirely lost."

When the *Ring* was mounted at Bayreuth in 1876, the story was quite different.

Friedrich Nietzsche, 1844-1900, Wagnerphile and author of The Birth of Tragedy from the Spirit of Music, *a work influenced by Wagner, which features a foreword about the composer*

Das Rheingold, *as staged in the new production at the Metropolitan Opera: Overleaf, Scene 3: in the bowels of the earth, Alberich (Franz Mazura) avariciously hovers over a portion of his hoard as Wotan (James Morris) asks what value gold can have in cheerless Nibelheim; Left, Scene 4: the giant Fasolt (John Macurdy), craving the companionship of Freia (Mari-Anne Häggander), informs Wotan that the goddess cannot be freed unless she is completely hidden from his sight by Alberich's treasure*

Joseph Bennett of the London *Daily Telegraph* reported, "Nothing more terribly real was ever put upon the stage…a series of representations unequaled for scenic truth and grandeur." The success was so great that even members of the orchestra were applauded in the streets as they walked from their lodgings to the theater.

Before long, Wagner began deploring his triumph. "People are fighting over the degree of my divinity," he snapped, and as for the Nibelungs, he added, "I've only got to hear the syllable *Ni* now to take to my heels!"

Once, regarding singers, Wagner said, "On the stage one wants brilliance; if there is no gold available, one takes silver, and if one hasn't got that, tin; but what one does not want is wood and leather." Among Wagner's "wood and leather" tenors was Ferdinand Jäger, whom the composer's wife Cosima called "poor, oblivious Herr Jäger." Nevertheless, at coffee time in Wahnfried, the Wagners' Bayreuth home, Jäger occasionally sang informally, with Wagner at the piano and the Master himself singing the role of Wotan.

One time in 1879 Jäger reported on *Götterdämmerung*'s remarkable success throughout Germany, though it was only three years since its premiere. "All other opera performances remain constantly empty," Jäger said. Wagner laughed, declaring, "So they're right when they say I'm ruining the theater. Where the *Ring* is being performed, people will go to see nothing else! Now the question remains how long the theaters can hold out before performing it. I could bring audiences back for the old operas too, by producing them myself as they ought to be done." Earlier he had condemned the illogic of French and Italian opera: "The mistake in the art form consists in this, that a means of expression (music) was made the end, and the end to be expressed (drama) was made a means."

Cosima Wagner wrote in her diary on May 8, 1881, regarding a performance of *Götterdämmerung* in Berlin that both husband and wife attended, "Despite all the deficiencies in the acting, R. and I are very moved by it; with Brünnhilde's last words we are leaning against each other, my head on his arm, and he exclaims to me, 'What we go through together!' He goes onstage and makes a speech."

Reminiscing among friends one evening in 1881, Wagner said, "God, when one thinks how I started, a provincial conductor with four first violins. What a joy to write for twelve and do oneself justice! I went farthest in the *Ring*, in order to reproduce effects of nature."

In later life, as Wagner mellowed, he insisted that his works "ought not to be judged by reason, but enjoyed through affection." He also conceded that for Siegfried and Brünnhilde he had asked "too much of a singer."

He stoutly resisted requests for explanations of the *Ring*, even from his friend August Röckel, a fellow anarchist from the Dresden barricades they had manned together in 1848. "It is wrong of you," he wrote, "to challenge me to explain it in words: you must feel that something is being enacted that is not to be expressed in mere words."

The Austrian-born soprano Amalie Materna, Brünnhilde for the original staging of Der Ring des Nibelungen at the Bayreuth Festival, 1876, and the first to sing the title role in Die Walküre at the Metropolitan Opera, 1885

Strolling in his garden one day, Wagner saw a blackbird and said it looked like Amalie Materna, creator of both the *Siegfried* and *Götterdämmerung* Brünnhildes as well as the *Parsifal* Kundry. "Birds with good voices are never particularly beautiful," he added. Sensitive to "ill-favored singers," Wagner passed over Marianne Brandt as Sieglinde for fear her plainness would impede Siegmund's onstage ardor. Both she—as Fricka—and Materna—as Brünnhilde in *Die Walküre*—later sang with great success in New York at the Metropolitan Opera.

Wagner himself staged the first integral production of *Der Ring des Nibelungen*, which inaugurated the Festival Theater at Bayreuth in 1876. Admission to the event was free, by invitation only, including a few seats at the back of the hall reserved "for the citizens of Bayreuth." The crush for tickets was unparalleled in the history of theater management.

One American violinist studying in Dresden at the time quickly learned the harp in order to see the performances as a member of the orchestra. She got the job, as the one woman amid five male harpists, only to find that from Wagner's "musical abyss," as he called the orchestra pit covered and hidden from view from audience and stage, she could see nothing.

Convinced that the theme of the four music dramas was "the curse of money and the disaster it brings," and vying for the privilege of performing before a panoply of kings and queens, as well as in the presence of virtually every important composer of Europe, star singers magnanimously waived their fees for this first *Ring*, content with only travel and living expenses. The $30,000 deficit at season's end dealt altruism a blow.

Caricature of Richard Wagner as conductor—"My baton will yet become the scepter of the future," he once said— published in London during 1876, when reports on the inauguration of the Bayreuth Festival were news

The year 1876 marked not only the first complete performance of *Der Ring des Nibelungen* at Bayreuth but also the 100th anniversary of America's independence. To celebrate both events, Theodore Steinway, head of his father's piano manufacturing business in Astoria, Queens, shipped Richard Wagner a complimentary Centennial Concert Grand, "the finest, most advanced and complicated musical instrument ever built."

Two years later, Steinway asked Wagner to send that same piano to the Steinway Central European Depot in Hamburg, so that the company's branch could install its latest mechanical invention, the Tone Pulsator. The composer happily complied with the request, and on March 11, 1879, he wrote from Bayreuth to New York, "I miss my Steinway grand as one misses a beloved wife; it is wanting constantly, wanting everywhere. I no longer indulge in music since that grand is gone, and trust its absence will not be too long protracted." He signed the letter "Very Truly Yours."

A few months later, after his piano was returned with its fancy new device, Wagner wrote Steinway again: "Though I do not possess the slightest dexterity in pianoforte playing, I delight in being able to do justice to your assumption of my inborn and cultivated sense of tone. For sounds of such beauty as those coming from my Steinway grand flatter and coax an agreeable tone picture from my harmonic senses." This letter he signed "Your Friend."

Alongside Edvard Grieg, Charles Gounod, Franz Liszt, Camille Saint-Saëns, Anton Bruckner and other composers, Peter Ilych Tchaikovsky attended the Bayreuth *Ring* of 1876. He was reporting for the *Russian Musical Gazette* and had just completed four operas of his own, including the most recent, *Cherevichki*, remembered today by old hands at the New York City Opera as *The Golden Slippers* and for the youthful Beverly Sills' performance as the heroine, Oxana.

Regarding *Das Rheingold*, Tchaikovsky wrote, "As a theatrical performance it interested and attracted me by its marvelous stage settings and production— as to the music, it is an impossible medley through which extremely beautiful and extraordinary details shimmer."

Six days later, he summed up his reactions: "Bayreuth has left a dismal impression.... On Thursday, with the last notes of *Götterdämmerung*, I felt free at last. Maybe the *Ring* is a great composition, but I have never heard anything so boring and so drawn out."

Verdi had stopped composing after *Aida*. In 1879, in answer to a friend's importuning, he wrote, "Why on earth should I write music? What should I succeed in doing? What have I to gain from it? The result would be wretched. I should be told all over again that I DON'T KNOW HOW TO WRITE, I have become a FOLLOWER OF WAGNER. A fine sort of glory! After a career of almost forty years to end up as an *imitator!*" Eight years later, he broke his silence at age seventy-four with *Otello*.

Brahms was another of the few living, major composers who did not attend the first Bayreuth *Ring*. Wagner had offended him by describing his music as "Handel, Mendelssohn and Schumann enveloped in leather." In 1876 Georg Henschel, later Sir George and a conductor of the Boston Symphony, took the score of *Götterdämmerung* to Brahms. "'Why did you bring it to me?' Brahms said. He had particularly asked me for it! 'The thing interests and fascinates one, and yet, properly speaking, is not always pleasant. With the *Tristan* score it is different. If I look at that in the morning, I am cross for the rest of the day.' I read out, from a Berlin paper, the news of the death at Bayreuth of a member of the Wagner orchestra. 'The first corpse,' said Brahms dryly."

Though Debussy described Wagner's *Ring* as "essentially a bundle of tricks," he nevertheless voyaged across the English Channel in 1903 to hear the tetralogy at Covent Garden conducted by Hans Richter, who had been decorated with the Order of Maximilian by the King of Bavaria and the Falcon Order by the Duke of Weimar after the Bayreuth Festival of 1876. The novelist Colette, reporting on the same event, wrote in her column for the *Gil Blas* newspaper, "I was throbbing, but I concealed my emotion like sensual desire."

Debussy, however, struck a dimmer note, saying in *Le Temps*, "Wagner never did anything of real service to music, and he never did much for Germany either.... He has awakened the secret thirst for the criminal in some of the most famous minds of our age." He interpreted Brünnhilde surrounded by a circle of fire as meaning "to destroy that scandalous legend that Jesus Christ died on the cross."

Maurice Ravel said that he would have been prouder to write Chabrier's *Le Roi Malgré Lui* than to have "written all of the *Ring*." Cosima Wagner, however, found Chabrier's predilection for music of the circus and fairground revealing "a whole world that makes you shudder."

The Academy of Music in New York announced a Grand Wagner Opera Festival starting March 12, 1877. *Die Walküre* was a disaster, despite three hours of rehearsal on the day of the performance and seven hours the preceding day. W.J. Henderson of the *Sun* called it "farcical," with Siegmund (A. Bischoff) in high-heeled sandals and floor-length fur jerkin, and the Ride of the Valkyries, billed as the "Walkueren Rite," consisting of projected lights by stereopticon.

Leopold Damrosch inaugurated the legendary seven seasons of German opera at the Metropolitan Opera (1884-91). The complete *Ring* was produced over a four-year span, beginning with *Die Walküre* in 1885, Anton Seidl presiding after Damrosch's death. The houses "were black with the vast audiences," and average receipts reached a capacity of $4,000 nightly. Critics agreed the season should be "chronicled in gold letters and stamped with the signature Richard Wagner." The backers, Ruppert's and Hell's Gate Breweries, were pleased.

Alfred Hertz

Nonetheless, audiences and critics pondered over the strange absence of choruses (how else is opera "grand," they asked) the endless passages devoid of the charm of a woman's voice (all those male duets and trios), the *Sprechstimme, Sprech-accent, Sprechsingen* and *Sprechgesang* that sounded to some like a "Wagnerian bark or shriek." They bridled at the immorality of the incest scene between Siegmund and Sieglinde.

Others complained of the house lights being lowered: "Finally, an American opera audience was last night compelled to sit during the representation in darkness so dense that neither shapely shoulders, gorgeous gown, nor dazzling diamonds could delight the eye."

George Bernard Shaw in 1892, two years before he ended his services to London as a music critic—for The Hornet *(1876-88),* The Star *(1888-90) and* The World *(1890-94) —and four years before his book* The Perfect Wagnerite *(1898)*

George Bernard Shaw, who began his career as a music critic, was a member of the Wagner Society and, in his own words, "ready to roll Wagner's log at all times." He was not above threatening his readers, as for instance when he wrote in 1894, "If *Der Ring des Nibelungen* is nothing to you but a newspaper phrase, then you are an ignoramus." Earlier, in 1889, he had declared, "Unless the audience hear and understand every word, five-sixths of the *Ring* will be voted a senseless bore."

As "Corno di Bassetto," his pen name at *The Star* in London, Shaw went to the July 1896 *Ring* at Bayreuth. He called *Die Walküre* a *succès de sommeil*, "endured by the average man because it contains four scenes for which he would sit out a Scotch sermon, or even a House of Commons debate."

As for *Siegfried*, Shaw noted that "Some of the Bayreuth artists rather excel in the art of making five minutes seem like twenty," adding "If any of the carpenters or gasmen backstage had botched his work last night as [tenor Wilhelm] Grüning several times botched his, he would be an unemployed man this morning."

Shaw was the first to point out that *Götterdämmerung*, which he translated as "Night Falls on the Gods," was opera, not "music drama." It has "all the operatic features excluded in *Das Rheingold*—choruses, finales, *scena* for the prima donna with the chorus looking on the way they did in [Rossini's] *Semiramide*…. The tenor, stabbed to death, comes to life to sing pretty things about his love before he finally expires just like Edgardo in *Lucia*. When two stalwart members of the chorus picked up The Slain Siegfried, and pretended to support him whilst he stood up and had a few more bars about Brynhild, it was impossible not to see that we had come round again to Valentin in Gounod's *Faust*."

Much later, in 1922, Shaw reflected differently on "Night Falls on the Gods." He recalled Wagner chanting in 1871 "Hail, hail, our Caesar born Wilhelm, Rock and Ward of German freedom," much in the way Englishmen in 1917 would shout "Hang, hang the Kaiser" about Wilhelm II, who had to seek safety in Holland. And he goes on to note, "Marx enthroned in Russia, pistolled Romanovs, fugitive Hapsburgs, exiled Hohenzollerns," all marking the ruins of empires, with Alberichs everywhere ruling the Nibelheim of "unregulated industrial capitalism."

In 1900 the first edition of Theodore Baker's *Dictionary of Musical Biographies* (proofread by Richard Aldrich, *The New York Times* music reviewer) proclaimed Richard Wagner "the grandest and most original dramatic composer of all times…*sui generis…facile princeps*." By 1902 what was called "The Great Race" began, with proponents and antagonists counting numbers of performances. The Paris Opera that year presented Wagner operas forty-four times, while the closest runner-up, Charles Gounod, accounted for forty-three. Berlin's Royal Opera performed Wagner thirty-seven times in a single season, eclipsing even Giacomo Meyerbeer, Wagner's quondam benefactor and later rival.

The face of music had changed, and musicians were worried. France's leading intellectual periodical, *Le Mercure*, invited "an investigation by artists, philosophers, critics and sociologists to determine whether German civilization had reached its zenith or whether it was destined to exert a still more potent influence in the future." The weight of their 1902 opinions favored France and Debussy's *Pelléas et Mélisande*.

Cosima Wagner, after attending a distressingly poor production of the *Ring* in 1878, made a prescient entry in her famous diary: "I shall alter all that when I produce *Die Walküre* in heaven at the right hand of God, and the old fellow and I are watching." She did not have to wait that long. Though it was unheard of in those days for a woman to produce or direct anything, thirteen years after the death of her husband, Cosima presented the *Ring* at Bayreuth in 1896, the second time in the history of the Festspielhaus that the tetralogy was mounted in its entirety. One of her first artistic choices was to hire her twenty-seven-year-old son, Siegfried Wagner, as conductor.

Together, Cosima and Siegfried attended rehearsals of Hans Richter and Felix Mottl, the other *Ring* maestros. Cosima would raise her deep and musical voice, which grew "very masculine in argument," as she made changes. She would turn to her son and say, "That was how the Master did it, don't you remember, Siegfried?" "I believe you are right, Mama," he would answer, though he had been seven years of age and absent from rehearsals for the three performances of the *Ring* in 1876.

She became the tyrannical *Frau Meisterin* without whose authority nothing Wagnerian could be done. Lilli Lehmann, the soprano who had been a Rhine-maiden in *Das Rheingold*, a Valkyrie in *Die Walküre* and the Forest Bird in *Siegfried* at the *Ring* premieres in 1876, when she returned in 1896 to portray the three Brünn-hildes, wrote of Cosima in her autobiography, *My Path Through Life*, "I suffered to see how the form of the *Ring*, which we had all so lovingly absorbed and taken away with us, together with our thoughts of its creator, was now being dislocated in the very place that was its home. All roads may lead to Rome, but to the Bayreuth of today there is but one—the road of slavish subjection. Cosima was not only very clever and well-informed. She also had assumed the authority of judgment peculiar to the aristocracy, so that what she announced was accepted as infallible."

George Bernard Shaw reviewed the 1896 *Ring* at Bayreuth. "The plain truth," he exclaimed, "is Madame Wagner does not know what acting can and cannot do, or how much the imagination of the audience will do when the situation goes beyond the resources of acting."

Everything had to be submitted to Cosima for approval at Bayreuth and even elsewhere. Before letting Geraldine Farrar sing the youthful Elsa in *Lohengrin* in Berlin, she made inquiries as to whether Farrar was "a flesh-and-blood virgin herself."

Her dominance over Bayreuth continued until 1906, when the doctor forbade her even to attend performances at Bayreuth, on the grounds that she became "too disturbed and agitated." She died at age ninety-three in 1930, and four months later her Fidi (Siegfried) collapsed during a rehearsal of *Götterdämmerung*.

Cosima Wagner (1837-1930), the composer's widow and daughter of Franz Liszt, photographed in 1900 when she ruled the Bayreuth Festival with an iron fist and willful hand— "My worry that I may overlook something must be constant," she confessed

Anton Seidl, who had worked under Wagner himself, copying out the score of the *Ring* and assisting at the first cycle in 1876—some said he was the composer's illegitimate son—came to the Metropolitan Opera in 1885 as a conductor. Among his credentials was a partitur of *Das Rheingold* inscribed to him by Wagner:

Everything in life is hollow
Surely it must therefore follow
When no bottle can be had
You must take a mug [Seidl] instead

Anton has alone succeeded
Everything he does is needed
He has entered to the core
Of the Nibelungen score

*Auguste Seidl-Kraus, the Metropolitan
Opera's original Sieglinde in* Die Walküre,
1885, Forest Bird in Siegfried, *1887, and Gutrune
in* Götterdämmerung, *1888, with her husband,
Anton Seidl, who conducted the first Ring cycle
mounted by the company, 1889, as well as
the Met premieres of* Das Rheingold,
Siegfried *and* Götterdämmerung

Die Walküre, *as staged in the new production
at the Metropolitan Opera:
Right, Act II: like an angel of death,
Brünnhilde (Hildegard Behrens) appears
before Siegmund to tell him he will soon
join other heroes in Valhalla;
Overleaf one, Act I: pursued by foes, the
wounded Siegmund (Peter Hofmann) finds
solace with the young wife of Hunding,
Sieglinde (Jeannine Altmeyer);
Overleaf two, Act II: as storm clouds
gather, the shocked and distressed
Brünnhilde (Hildegard Behrens) learns of
the torments that tear at her father,
Wotan, chief of the gods (Simon Estes)*

Seidl led the first American performances of the complete *Ring* and toured five cities with it in 1889. The cast was something of a family affair. Seidl was married to Auguste Seidl-Kraus, the Woodbird and Sieglinde. Victor Herbert, a cellist in the orchestra, married another, non-Wagnerian diva, Theresa Herbert-Förster. And Lilli Lehmann, the Brünnhilde, had her tenor husband, Paul Kalisch, stand in when better tenors were indisposed.

Seidl's *Ring* began March 4 and ended on March 11, 1889, after which the Metropolitan Opera Orchestra rewarded him with a *Tusch*, an instrumental flourish. The occasion was greeted by "the mellow sound of gratulation by kid gloves... swelled to sharp applause as bare hands got into the act."

Maurice Grau, the Met's general manager at the turn of the century, was first to coin one of those truisms that are not so true. He said, "Wagner will draw even without good scenery." Some critics at first decried Wagner's scenic effects and questioned his "employing in serious drama mechanical devices of a kind that custom associates only with children's pantomimes and idle spectacles." Eduard Hanslick, the all-powerful German critic who insisted that "Music expresses musical ideas and can express no others," scoffed at any composer such as Wagner, "whose creativity in the *Ring* depended on the invention of the electric light, the harp and the bass tuba."

But while audiences' pulses quickened, eyes goggled and minds boggled, critics still delighted in mocking the demands Wagner made on stagecraft. Staid old H.E. Krehbiel of the *Tribune* recounted the plot of *Siegfried* for his readers: "A bear is brought on to frighten a dwarf; a dragon sings, vomits forth steam from his cavernous jaws, fights and dies with a kindly and prophetic warning to his slayer, and a bird becomes endowed with the gift of articulate speech...." Another said point-blank, "*Das Rheingold* has the same species of attractiveness as a Christmas pantomime of the old kind, with its fairy-talk and marvelous pictures of No-Man's Land."

With its dwarfs, giants, gods and humans surrounded by thunder, lightning, rainbow, river, moonlight, flames, clouds, sunshine and forest murmurs, the *Ring* is a mare's nest of possible mishaps. Even so simple an object as an anvil is troublesome. To begin with, how can the prop men produce an anvil light enough to be portable, yet substantial enough to emit a sound more solid than a tinkle? Once found, what guarantees are there that said anvil will split in two as required? Many a Siegfried's anvil has resisted every blandishment. Recently at the Met, Wolfgang Neumann's fell apart before he touched it with his sword. Neumann became something of a hero when the head of Siegfried's forging hammer flew off into space. "Barely skipping a beat, he ran over [and] seized another one from the hearth," one awed critic wrote. But Neumann's troubles were not over that season. At the next performance, the hammer stayed together but the rope-pulled bellows stuck. He had to sing and turn sidewise each time to fan the forge's flame by hand.

During 1906, one *Siegfried* mishap added to stage realism. Siegfried, a particularly vigorous swordsman, six-foot-four in height, dealt the dragon Fafner so energetic and deft a blow that it knocked unconscious the lone stagehand inside, operating the jaws and flapping ears, "whereupon he rolled over in so realistic a manner as to deserve special applause." Today's high-tech *Wurm* at the Met requires six men inside, working its arms, mouth and single eye.

Steam pipes and steam curtain, essential for scene changes in *Das Rheingold* and for the magic fire in *Die Walküre* and *Götterdämmerung*, used to make the theater smell like a laundry. Even nowadays they act erratically, once flooding the stage with water instead of "smoke."

DIE WALKÜRE

Problematical always are animals, as any stage manager will tell. Wagner, with his ram-drawn chariot and troop of horses, defied the limits of practicality. The sacred steed Grane, whom Brünnhilde apostrophizes in Siegfried and to whom the last minutes of Götterdämmerung are addressed, poses a horny dilemma. When onstage, he may neigh, shy or otherwise misbehave. When he is absent, prima donnas, with their bagfuls of sugar cubes, complain.

Kirsten Flagstad, the famous Norwegian Brünnhilde, liked to recount the story of how the stable owner who had been supplying her Grane for one opera house went bankrupt. The bailiffs locked all the horses up. Close to midnight in the last act of Siegfried, when Brünnhilde awakened, there was still no Grane—a fact that upset the literal-minded Flagstad. Not even her Wunderstimme, she felt, could conjure up a horse in the imagination of the audience. As she reached the line "Dort seh' ich Grane," however, in trotted "a really lovely horse, very well behaved." A policeman on duty outside the opera house had heard of the diva's distress and gallantly dismounted for the finale.

Birgit Nilsson, Flagstad's Swedish successor as the Valkyrie, after a series of symbolic light projection productions in Europe, sighed with relief when she arrived at the old Met for the 1961 revival of Götterdämmerung, exclaiming "At last I can sing to a real horse."

Alfred Hertz, dominant conductor of German repertory for thirteen years at the Metropolitan, beginning in 1902, and for fifteen years at the San Francisco Symphony beginning in 1915, was nearsighted. Once he wanted to catch a rehearsal of Act II of Die Walküre to check on his assistant's guidance of the orchestra. Peering at the stage as he entered the general manager's box at the Met, he asked, "Who's the Brünnhilde?" One of the occupants quickly piped up, "I'm not sure, but I think it's the lady standing on the rock."

One of Hertz' most reliable tenors, Andreas Dippel—later co-manager in charge of the German repertory for two seasons with Giulio Gatti-Casazza—used to dispose of singing aspirants by recommending them to study certain nonexistent roles. For bass-baritones he recommended Wotan in Götterdämmerung: there he sits without uttering a sound.

Jean De Reszke, the elegant Polish tenor who sang both Siegfrieds at the Metropolitan Opera during the Gay Nineties, balancing appearances in such heroic roles with performances of Gounod's lyrical Faust and Roméo

Lillian Nordica, Yankee diva from Maine, was trained by Cosima Wagner in the three Brünnhilde roles. Twenty-four hours after Die Walküre, she sang Violetta in La Traviata. At age forty-six in 1903, Nordica sang the Walküre Brünnhilde and two days later the one in Götterdämmerung, followed four days later by Marguerite in Faust.

Versatile as she was, she excelled as the preeminent Wagner soprano of her generation. She initiated a grandiose project of Bayreuth-on-the-Hudson at Harmon, New York. At the tree-planting ceremony, she said, "My favorite tree has always been tree-mendous applause.... At my funeral," she added, "I want a baritone to sing Wotan's farewell and an orchestra to play the funeral march from Götterdämmerung. For me that music has such dear memories. And then I want some great speaker to say, 'She did her damnedest!'"

Jean De Reszke, "incomparable" tenor of the French and Italian repertory, was the first major non-German to sing Wagner in German and to reveal that such music could be "beautifully sung." On December 30, 1896, at the Metropolitan Opera, De Reszke for his first Siegfried chose to emphasize the hero's youthfulness and appeared clean-shaven. Responding to audience protests, the management asked him to grow back at least his mustache.

Die Walküre, as staged in the new production at the Metropolitan Opera:
Overleaf, Act III: the Valkyries, Wotan's warrior daughters, gathered on a mountain peak, try to defend their sister Brünnhilde from their father's wrath;
Left, Act III: as flames surround the Valkyries' Rock, where Brünnhilde (Hildegard Behrens) has been placed in sleep, Wotan (Simon Estes) proclaims the mountaintop inviolate to all save a fearless hero

That night also marked Nellie Melba's first and only stab at a Wagner role. According to David Bispham, the American baritone playing Alberich in the same performance, De Reszke "in the heavy fur coat of Siegfried patrolled the forward part of the stage to keep the white-clad Melba from rushing to the footlights, over which she had so many times sung to delighted audiences." In any event, Melba's voice of pearls and velvet gave way under the strain of Wagner's surging orchestra, and she soon vacated the stage for a year. Five years after that Siegfried, De Reszke's voice also failed. Wagner was blamed for both "vocal suicides."

Ernestine Schumann-Heink, one of the first Metropolitan singing stars to become a household name, was "Mother Schumann" to millions of Americans. Her finest role was Erda, spirit or goddess of the earth—Mother Earth, or *ewiges Weib* (Eternal Woman), Brünnhilde's mother by Wotan. Cosima Wagner called her "Erda" offstage as well as on, so deep was the singer's association with the role. She took her leave from the Met as Erda in *Siegfried* in 1932 at the age of seventy, after more than half a century of public singing.

Schumann-Heink had been inspired to sing by Marianne Brandt, whom Wagner much admired, despite her looks, and Schumman-Heink was comforted by the plainness of face she shared, claiming that "All contraltos should be homely."

Olivia Fremstad changed her name to Olive so that it would have thirteen letters, just like Richard Wagner's. The numerology worked: for eleven years at the Metropolitan Opera, 1903 to 1914, she was the yardstick by which Wagner sopranos were measured.

Fremstad's long and bitter rivalry with another prima donna of the era, Johanna Gadski, reached its apex during a Met performance of *Die Walküre*. Fremstad appeared as Sieglinde on this occasion, with Gadski as Brünnhilde. After Act II, Fremstad came offstage, her forearm streaming with blood, but she shook off any assistance. "Gadski did this on purpose," she hissed. "She dragged my arm right across the nails of her breastplate. She wanted to keep me from bowing with her." Whereupon Fremstad powdered her nose, arranged her wig and took the curtain call, smiling, gracious, holding Gadski's hand so that blood dripped on the other soprano's sleeve. Gadski glared, Fremstad glared back, but to the audience they seemed sugar sweet.

At the Vienna State Opera in 1928, Maria Jeritza announced, "I have the most beautiful elbows in the world," and explained that she bathed them in grapefuit juice every morning. That evening she sang Sieglinde in *Die Walküre*, dressed in a long white silk dress with trailing train. In those days opera stars provided their own costumes.

Act II, Jeritza waited in the wings as Maria Olczewska, the Fricka, harangued Wotan. Bored, or deliberately wicked, Jeritza began whispering and giggling with Siegmund so noisily that Olczewska turned and spat all the way from center stage almost into the wings. The joking stopped, but Olczewska was fired, went to Chicago and made a long, distinguished career, singing anywhere Jeritza was not.

Frida Leider, who rejuvenated American interest in the *Ring* with her Chicago debut in 1928, suffered both World Wars in her native Germany. In World War I she counted out potatoes with her mother as carefully as if they had been diamonds, and her most cherished gift from a fan then was a half pound of butter, handed her after singing the *Walküre* Brünnhilde in 1918 in Königsberg. In 1945 she was living in Pausin, twenty-five miles outside Berlin,

where she had concealed a floor-length ermine coat in the basement of her house and had buried her jewelry in the garden. A contingent of victorious soldiers ran into her house demanding "keys to the safe!" They searched the place and were about to leave when one of the officers' chauffeurs noticed a painting of Leider as Brünnhilde in helmet, shield, spear and cuirass. "Soldier!" he cried and aimed his pistol at her. "Artista, artista!" she sang, and was saved.

Not long after, Russian soldiers ransacked her house in Pausin. They had mistaken it for the doctor's clinic next door and were looking for condoms. The Russians soon began issuing food rations to members of the Berlin State Opera, and in 1946 Geraldine Farrar began sending her food parcels. But Leider's voice, which once had ranged over two and a half octaves, with all registers available at full volume over the surf of the Wagner orchestra, was gone. She was fifty-eight.

Danish heldentenor Lauritz Melchior, the Metropolitan Opera's indispensable Siegfried, 1925-49, between scenes with Marek Windheim, a frequent Mime of the 1930s

Hearty, healthy and athletic Lauritz Melchior, with the huge, baritonally colored tenor voice that dominated the Wagner repertory at the Metropolitan Opera for twenty-five years, until 1950, was always hungry. He had shot—and eaten—the deer whose skin became his costume for Siegmund. He confided to friends, "The thought of a good meal incites me to my finest performances." Duck stuffed with Waldorf Salad was his favorite entree. He also loved the game of skat and passed long waits between entrances playing cards with colleagues. (Kirsten Flagstad always knitted.) When the warning bell sounded, he called for his dresser. On occasion, this passion got Melchior into trouble.

Once for Act II of *Götterdämmerung* he forgot in his haste to put on the Ring. Thanks to a member of the chorus and some odd positioning onstage of the singers, the Ring reached Siegfried's hand in time for Brunnhilde's line "Einen Ring sah' ich an deiner Hand." "Kleinchen," Melchior's wife, berated him for his zeal at cards, in reply to which Melchior tossed off a high note, and the matter was forgotten.

During another *Götterdämmerung*, this time in the last act, Frida Leider was Brünnhilde to Melchior's Siegfried. When Leider leaned over Siegfried's corpse to remove the Ring from his hand, the Ring was there, but Melchior wasn't. He was in the wings, smiling, in a dinner jacket, ready for the after-opera supper awaiting them. Siefgried's body was being played by a member of the chorus. When Melchior tried to come onstage for a curtain call, Leider said a very firm "No!"

Kirsten Flagstad made her debut at the Metropolitan Opera on a Saturday matinee broadcast of *Die Walküre*, February 2, 1935. As Quaintance Eaton in *The Miracle of the Met* put it, "Audiences went wild and became Wagnerites overnight." She was thirty-nine years old and had set about learning all three Brünnhildes for the first time. Sibelius pronounced her best as the *Walküre* Brünnhilde, since the role matched her "Nordic goddess temperament."

Flagstad revitalized Wagner at the Met and helped keep the house solvent during the Depression. In the 1950s, Rudolf Bing called her "the Caruso of our time," referring both to her voice and to her ticket-selling ability. She was known as "the Battleship" for her indestructibility. After a performance she sometimes made unwary admirers feel her thighs to show the tension still clinging to her leg muscles from standing still so long and reaching all those top Cs hurled toward the gallery.

Not only was a rose named after Flagstad, but Ogden Nash immortalized her in poetry as "the singer from Scandinavia, land of peace and sane behavia."

Though Kirsten Flagstad confessed to being tempted to sleep during the magic fire music of *Die Walküre*, while Brünnhilde lies supine for half an hour onstage, her successor at the Met, Helen Traubel, the St. Louis Woman who had never set foot outside America, actually did sleep. Traubel of the peaches-and-cream complexion and red-blond hair turned to designer Adrian of Hollywood for her first *Götterdämmerung* Brünnhilde, in 1942. To accent her six-foot height and suggest the "exuberance of a young goddess," he costumed her in an ankle-length gray skirt and long blue cape, perfect for her rather static stage deportment, somewhat less so for the sense of the opera.

Traubel shared with Lauritz Melchior a distaste for rehearsing. On one occasion when the soprano sent an understudy to pace or mark her stage positions, general manager Rudolf Bing said, "Very well, but the understudy does the performance too." Conductor Max Rudolf, however, never minded Melchior's absences because, he said, after 1,100 performances in Wagner, "He can be trusted to make the same mistakes each time."

Both Melchior and Traubel left the Met in disputes with Bing, he in 1950, she in 1953. The divo went to Hollywood, the diva to night clubs, where she sang the Toreador Song and "Vesti la giubba," or to television, where she appeared with Jimmy Durante. She also wrote a mystery novel, *The Metropolitan Opera Murders*. Wishful thinking, one wonders.

Siegfried Wagner, in his autobiography *Werk und Wiedergabe* (Work and Reconstruction), published in 1929, characterized himself: "Siegfried was the name my parents gave me. Well, I have smashed no anvils, killed no dragons and waded through no seas of flame. All the same, I hope to have been not unworthy of my name, for at least I am not given to fear."

Winifred Williams, an English girl adopted by pianist Karl Klindworth who made the still-used piano transcriptions of the *Ring*, was eighteen when she married forty-six-year-old Siegfried, Wagner's son. At Siegfried's death in 1930 she, first of the family who had not actually known *der Meister*, assumed control of Bayreuth. Sharing the Wagnerian conviction of German cultural supremacy was an obscure politician, Adolf Hitler, who made pilgrimages to Bayreuth and whose favorite opera was *Rienzi*, though based on a novel by another foreigner, Bulwer-Lytton.

Responding to Hitler's taste for "maximum realistic visual splendor," Winifred's Bayreuth became something of a Nazi allegory. Siegfried reforged his father's sword (broken by the defeat of World War I) in the face of opposition from Fafner (international banking), and awakened Brünnhilde (Germany).

Much as Wagner in his lifetime had been likened to Christ (to which the composer always replied with a polite "Thank you"), and his scene painter Paul von Joukowsky had painted a family portrait with Wagner as Joseph, Cosima as Mary and little Siegfried as the infant Jesus, popular postcards of the thirties showed Hitler as Siegfried, sword in hand, bestriding the world.

When Arturo Toscanini in 1931 swept the dust of Bayreuth from his heels, Winifred Wagner asked Hitler to write a personal letter trying to persuade the Maestro to return. In 1933, Hitler became Chancellor of the Third Reich and authorized 50,000 marks annually for Bayreuth out of his personal, tax-exempt funds. Winifred put the money to good use. Where Wagner had twenty-six male singers for the Gibichungs in Act II of *Götterdämmerung*, Winifred and conductor Heinz Tietjen had a chorus of 101. She nixed, however, the suggestion that the shields of the Gibichungs be painted with swastikas.

Hitler contemplated marrying Winifred. His identification with the heroic Siegfried as symbol ended in 1945, when he looked more like Wotan "sowing with his own hands the seeds of his undoing." In 1947, the denazification court placed Winifred on the list of major collaborators, depriving her of control over Bayreuth. She withdrew from her inheritance in favor of her sons Wieland, age thirty, and Wolfgang, twenty-eight.

Siegfried Wagner—like his father a composer-conductor-designer-director—and his bride, Winifred, not long after their marriage, September 22, 1915

As the Greek work of art expressed the spirit of a splendid nation, the work of art of the future is intended to express the spirit of free people, irrespective of all national boundaries; the national element in it must be no more than an ornament, an added individual charm, and not a confining boundary."
RICHARD WAGNER
Art and Revolution, 1848

In 1945, at the end of World War II in Europe, when the U.S. Army occupied Germany and turned Bayreuth's Festspielhaus, a theater built for a devoted minority, into a vaudeville house for the majority, some items—steer horns, alp horns and the like—were confiscated as souvenirs by the GIs. A more serious loss from the archives was the final copy of the *Walküre* full score, presented by Wagner to King Ludwig of Bavaria. Left intact, however, in the hallway through which artists pass on their way to the stage, was a passe-partout glass framing of a Wagner autograph that reads, "Take care of the little notes: the big ones will take care of themselves." This was Wagner's last written instruction to his singers before the opening of the *Ring* in 1876.

Richard Wagner's grandson Wieland in 1951 reopened Bayreuth after a seven-year hiatus with economical productions, rid of "national associations" and revealing their "universal psychology." A brilliant *homme de théâtre*, he wrote his own epitaph several years before his death in 1966: "Here lies Wagner, who is nothing. He has never received a knighthood of the meanest kind. He has not been able to coax a cur from behind a stove…nor a degree from any university." When Wieland took over direction of Bayreuth in 1949, he explained "Valhalla is Wall Street," meaning that wealth and power should not be left in private hands.

Birgit Nilsson, who dominated Valhalla for a quarter of a century at both Bayreuth and the Met, established an unexpected rapport with Richard Wagner when she juxtaposed in her pictorial autobiography a photo of her granitic profile next to the composer's own. The resemblance was more than striking—it was identical.

With the advent of long-playing records in 1950 and the invention of stereophony six years later, the possibility of a complete recording of the *Ring* became reality. The old 78rpm discs, with less than five minutes' playing time, would have required 224 sides to encompass the cycle's sixteen hours. When Decca London's recording director, John Culshaw, set about realizing the stupendous project in 1958, he persuaded Kirsten Flagstad to come out of retirement to sing Fricka in *Das Rheingold*. Flagstad's sixty-three-year-old voice, yet powerful and still with its diamond-cutting edge, had lost its high C. "I would certainly like to record the *Walküre* Fricka, and can see your point in wanting me to," she wrote to Culshaw, also agreeing to record Waltraute, a mezzo Valkyrie in *Götterdämmerung*, with Birgit Nilsson as Brünnhilde. Upon Flagstad's death in 1962, those roles were awarded to Christa Ludwig, who has since gone on to participate in two other complete *Ring* recordings.

Another Culshaw casting coup was Joan Sutherland as *Siegfried*'s Forest Bird. He also managed to get Dietrich Fischer-Dieskau for the chief of the Gibichungs in *Götterdämmerung*— Gunther, "a weak character with very little rewarding music to sing and usually sung by second-class baritones." As for the Brünnhilde, Birgit Nilsson, after "Heil dir, Sonne!"—her awakening, and the ensuing impassioned

Prominent Ring artists at the Metropolitan Opera 1940-60:
Above: Blanche Thebom as Fricka;
Top row, opposite page: Kerstin Thorborg as Waltraute, Norman Cordon as Hunding, Rose Bampton as Sieglinde, Helen Traubel as Brünnhilde;
Second row: Astrid Varnay as Sieglinde, Jarmila Novotna as Freia, Joel Berglund as Wotan, Gerhard Pechner as Alberich;
Third row: Herbert Janssen as Gunther, Regina Resnik as Gutrune, Set Svanholm as Siegfried, Jean Madeira as Erda;
Bottom row: Peter Klein as Mime, Margaret Harshaw as Brünnhilde, Ramon Vinay as Siegmund, Hermann Uhde as Wotan

love duet in *Siegfried*, the most exhausting thirty-five minutes in opera—conductor Georg Solti cried, "It's *animalig*! It's perfect screaming!" adding tactfully that he meant her voice had "the right earthy, animal quality of love and joy."

The animosity between Rudolf Bing and conductor/producer Herbert Von Karajan has been well documented. Perhaps it started in Vienna, when the maestro announced it had taken him eight full-length lighting rehearsals to attain a certain "Wagnerian gloom." Bing was widely quoted as saying, "I could have got it that dark in one."

When Karajan came to Bing's Metropolitan in 1967 to supervise his own staging of the *Ring* with Günther Schneider-Siemssen's multitudinous light projections, during one rehearsal Karajan ordered his assistant, "More light on Wotan." According to union rules, the assistant repeated this to the lighting director, who in turn relayed it to the electrician backstage. Over the microphone came the query, "Who is Wotan?" Bing hurriedly left the auditorium.

At one rehearsal, Birgit Nilsson dispelled the prevailing Karajan gloom by reporting onstage in a miner's hat equipped with lamp. The conductor was not amused, though Bing was. Later, while practicing *Götterdämmerung*, she was victim of an accident on the dark stage, falling through a trap door and dislocating a shoulder. Despite pain, Nilsson sang in the premiere.

Vincent Sheean, in *First and Last Love*, his book of musical reminiscences, wondered at the distortions the *Ring* has survived over the century of its existence. "It lends itself to interpretation with the ease of the Sphinx and the plausibility of the Mona Lisa."

Faubion Bowers, a native of Oklahoma, studied at Columbia, Juilliard, the Ecole Normale de Musique in Paris and at Nichigo Bunka Gakko of Tokyo. With six languages at his command, he has penned books on Scriabin, Japanese theater, dance in India and Russian music. He is also a contributor to virtually every major American publication, from Vogue *to* The Village Voice *to* Opera News.

Birgit Nilsson in miner's hat, ready to light up the stage as Brünnhilde during a rehearsal for Herbert Von Karajan's new production of Die Walküre *at the Metropolitan Opera, 1967*

Siegfried, *as staged in the new production at the Metropolitan Opera: Right, Act I: at an anvil, Siegfried (Wolfgang Neumann) repairs the weapon; Overleaf one, Act I: Mime (Horst Hiestermann) plays a duel of wits with an aged Wanderer (Donald McIntyre), who poses three enigmas to the gnome; Overleaf two, Act II: deep in the forest, after Siegfried has killed Fafner, Alberich (Franz Mazura) and Mime (Horst Hiestermann) argue over the Nibelung treasure in the dragon's cave*

SIEGFRIED

THE RING: 100 YEARS AT THE MET

by Frank Merkling

The 1988-89 season at the Metropolitan Opera has a centennial ring to it: it was exactly 100 years ago that Richard Wagner's monumental cycle *Der Ring des Nibelungen* first was performed in America. The first uncut *Ring* at the Met followed a decade later. There have been only five different Met productions of the cycle all told, the current one included, and as of 1988-89, Günther Schneider-Siemssen became the first set designer entrusted with two of them.

The Met's new *Ring* is also the first to be led by an American-born conductor. The casts James Levine is working with this season include Americans, notably Jessye Norman as Sieglinde, Jeannine Altmeyer as Brünnhilde, James Morris as Wotan. So the forging of this latest *Ring* marks more than a hollow anniversary. It attests to the coming of age of the native-born artist as interpreter of Wagner's masterwork on home soil, if not yet in the common language.

Actually, an American conducting the *Ring* cycle is more of a novelty than Americans singing in one or another of the *Ring* operas. Annie Louise Cary was portraying Wagner heroines in her native land prior to the opening of the original Metropolitan Opera House in 1883, and she was followed at Thirty-ninth Street and Broadway by a line of distinguished countrymen and -women. There were David Bispham as Alberich in *Das Rheingold* and *Siegfried* and as Wotan in *Die Walküre*, Emma Eames as Sieglinde opposite Lillian Nordica as Brünnhilde, Louise Homer as Waltraute in *Götterdämmerung*. Later there was the naturalized Olive Fremstad as Sieglinde, the three Brünnhildes and the *Rheingold* Fricka.

Later still came Clarence Whitehill, "the foremost Wagnerian among American male singers," who first sang Wotan at the Met in 1909-10. It was Whitehill who put his finger on a problem already beginning to manifest itself in those relaxed days before World War I. "I am coming to the conclusion," he told an interviewer, "that to sing heavy bass operatic roles continuously against the immense modern orchestra must in the end impair the voice more or less." Many a later singer would agree.

It was not the orchestra's size alone that could be faulted here. After all, it had remained the same since Wagner first wrote his scores. The problem was the way the orchestra increasingly was being conducted. Large opera houses require a large sound—or there is a temptation to think they do. With the advent of dynamic

Vienna-born Artur Bodanzky, who from 1915 until 1939 conducted all performances of Der Ring des Nibelungen *at the Metropolitan Opera*

Siegfried, as staged in the new production at the Metropolitan Opera:
Overleaf, Act III, Scene 1: the omniscient Erda (Anne Gjevang), confronted by the Wanderer, tries to avoid his questions about the fate of the gods, after which Siegfried (Wolfgang Neumann), seeking the summit where Brünnhilde rests, encounters the god (Donald McIntyre); Left, Act III, Scene 2: roused from her long slumber by Siegfried's kiss, Brünnhilde (Hildegard Behrens) reawakens to life, hailing the sun and her hero

maestros such as Gustav Mahler and Arturo Toscanini shortly after the turn of the century, the days of the orchestra as mere permissive accompanist were numbered. The essence of Wagnerian drama was transferred from stage to pit, where the composer had intended it to be all along. If that pit remained uncovered, unlike the one at the Festspielhaus in Bayreuth, who could say this was not necessary to reach an audience of nearly 4,000, as opposed to one of less than 2,000?

Herbert Von Karajan could say it. Indeed, Karajan has made a point of conducting as if there *were* a covered pit. His productions of the four *Ring* operas at the Salzburg Easter Festival during the late '60s set the style for the Met's own subsequent productions, sonically as well as scenically. They relied less on supervoices, though Birgit Nilsson sang Brünnhilde in them, and less on elaborately constructed settings, such as Lee Simonson's of 1947-48. It was Simonson who designed that last investiture of the cycle at the Met prior to the first Schneider-Siemssen *Ring* of 1968-74.

In the Karajan philosophy of *Ring* staging, lighting and projections came to mean more than painted canvas flats or even sculptural "symbolic" scenery in the manner of such early-in-the-century designers as Adolphe Appia and Gordon Craig. This type of approach, cinematic rather than mechanistic, had been introduced by Wieland Wagner in his epochal Bayreuth stagings of the early 1950s. No longer would it be acceptable for the Rhinemaidens, for example, to be trundled about on carts or flown from breeches buoys to simulate swimming. Illusion had grown more sophisticated.

Before Karajan, who served as his own stage director, there had to come other worthy maestros. Alfred Hertz conducted a new *Ring* cycle in 1913-14 to mark the centenary of Wagner's birth, and Artur Bodanzky conducted at least one uncut cycle every year from 1929 to 1939. Sets came from the Kautsky brothers of Vienna. It was Bodanzky who stood on the podium that afternoon in the depths of the Depression when Kirsten Flagstad made her debut as Sieglinde, ushering in an age as golden, in retrospect, as that of the pre-Valhalla gods. Most often her invincible hero onstage was Lauritz Melchior—a Siegmund and Siegfried for the ages.

It is important to remember, as Philip L. Miller wrote recently in *Opera News*, that "before Kirsten Flagstad there was Frida Leider, before Karin Branzell (as Erda) and Kerstin Thorborg (as Fricka) there was Margarete Matzenauer, before Friedrich Schorr there was Whitehill." In other words, outstanding singing actors and actresses did exist on the Met's Wagner roster before February 2, 1935. And the breed did not become extinct with World War II. Along came an American soprano named Helen Traubel, and another named Astrid Varnay.

It was Traubel who sang all three Brünnhildes in that Simonson postwar *Ring*, made possible by a gift of $100,000 from the Metropolitan Opera Guild. (The next *Ring* production, two decades later, would cost Eastern Airlines five times as much.) The work of a Broadway designer rather than a German or an Austrian as heretofore, it signaled the arrival of the American in areas of opera besides performing. Moreover, though it had "realism" of a jaggedly stylized sort, this production reflected the industrial dynamic of the Bauhaus and Art Moderne rather than the Nordic Eddas of yore. It spoke of renewed optimism in a postwar world.

One wonders if the annual *Ring* cycles of the 1930s, presented in the imported, traditional sets of 1913-14, didn't owe their popularity as much to a need for a Never-Never Land as to the enthusiasm of a Bodanzky or an onstage team such as Flagstad and Melchior. Like the musical films of another unbeatable team, Fred Astaire and Ginger Rogers, these mythic operas offered an escape from the grim reality of bread lines and unemployment. So they filled one of the several roles defined by the pianist-educator Ernest Hutcheson in his *Musical Guide to the Ring* (1940):

Sets designed by Lee Simonson for Der Ring des Nibelungen at the Metropolitan Opera, 1947-48: Top row: Das Rheingold Scene 4 and Die Walküre Act I; Second row: Die Walküre Act II and Siegfried Act I; Third row: Siegfried Acts II and III; Fourth row: Götterdämmerung Act I, Scene 1, and Act II; Below: Swedish tenor Set Svanholm with Austrian conductor Fritz Stiedry at the time of their joint debuts with the company, a 1946 Siegfried

It is possible to look at the *Ring* in many lights. We may accept it, as no doubt many do, simply as gorgeous music accompanied by spectacular stage effects and a grandiose story. We may think of it as a medley of fairy tales, in which we encounter giants and a giant-killer, a sleeping beauty, a magic ring, sword and helmet, mysterious charms and spells of incredible potency, a talking bird, a youth who sets out to learn to shiver, and so forth. Or, on a higher plane, we may find in it an interpretation in operatic terms of the vivid Northern mythology rooted in the Icelandic sagas and the German Nibelungenlied. We may see in it, as Shaw did, a social treatise on the vexed relations between capital and labor. We might even read into it a homily on the text that the love of money is the root of all evil.

Certainly the last two of these implications were picked up by Patrice Chéreau in his controversial *Ring* production for Bayreuth in 1976, for which Pierre Boulez provided quicksilver orchestral support. Chéreau's visual approach was postmodern, using "quotations" from the past for expressive effect, in this case styles ranging from the late eighteenth century all the way up to the 1920s and beyond.

Fritz Lang had a similar end in view when he made his two-part 1923 film *Siegfrieds Tod* (Wagner's original title for the *Ring* project), which Hitler greatly admired. It was a dipping into the glorious past to bolster up an uncertain present. Thus each era seems to seize on one or another aspect of the *Ring* in order to make a point of its own. Eras of relative prosperity, such as ours or the one in which Shaw was writing, can afford to see Wagner's tetralogy as an attempt to make us change our ways, while depressed eras may seek refuge in the myth.

Can one say, therefore, that *Der Ring des Nibelungen* means all things to all men? One can, at the risk of overlooking the fact that the different *Ring* operas have also led a life at the Met apart from their siblings, or at least some of them have. *Das Rheingold*, the favorite child of many by virtue of its vivid swiftness and economy of music as well as text, has been performed by itself less often than any of the others, even *Götterdämmerung*. (Opera audiences do enjoy an intermission, and *Das Rheingold* is supposed to be given without one—not always the case in Met history.) *Siegfried*, in which most of the *Ring*'s fairytale aspects are to be found, has always been popular. But most popular of all, even to the point of rating a new production by itself, designed by Jonel Jorgulesco in 1935-36, is *Die Walküre*, with its tragic love story on two levels.

We are concerned here, however, with the *Ring* as a cycle. That is what's special, what's centennial, what's phenomenal even: "the longest interrelated series of musical compositions in existence." Metropolitan Operagoers of 1988-89 are privileged to experience this great artistic unity uncut, with casts that are homegrown as well as imported, in an investiture that shows the accumulated insights of a designer, Schneider-Siemssen, and director, Otto Schenk, who know Wagner, his ways, his origins. And the conductor is an American from Cincinnati, where many Germans settled to take up, as the *Ring* has, a new life in the New World.

Frank Merkling was Editor in Chief of Opera News *from 1957 until 1974, responsible for 427 separate editions of the magazine. He is co-author of* The Golden Horseshoe, *a history of the old Met, published in 1965, and has written for* House and Garden, Musical America *and* Collier's Encyclopedia.

Prominent Ring artists at the Metropolitan Opera 1960-80:
Above: Jon Vickers as Siegmund;
Top row, opposite page: Birgit Nilsson as Brünnhilde, Leonie Rysanek as Sieglinde, Jerome Hines as Wotan, George London as Wotan;
Second row: Gottlob Frick as Hagen, Hans Hopf as Siegfried, Mignon Dunn as Waltraute, Karl Ridderbusch as Hunding;
Third row: Régine Crespin as Brünnhilde, Thomas Stewart as Wotan, Christa Ludwig as Fricka, Gundula Janowitz as Sieglinde;
Bottom row: Zoltán Kelemen as Alberich, Sherrill Milnes as Donner, Jess Thomas as Siegfried, Gerhard Stolze as Mime

A RING BOOKSHELF

by David Hamilton

Régisseur Herbert Von Karajan, Salzburg-born conductor for the company's mountings of Die Walküre *and* Das Rheingold, *1967-69*

Sets designed by Günther Schneider-Siemssen for Der Ring des Nibelungen *at the Metropolitan Opera, 1967-74: Top row:* Das Rheingold *Scenes 1 and 4; Second row:* Die Walküre *Acts I and III; Third row:* Siegfried *Acts I and II; Fourth row:* Götterdämmerung *Act I, Scene 1, and Act II*

In recent years the already bulging library shelves devoted to Wagner have grown steadily fatter, especially with new translations and original works in English, among them two welcome, concise introductions to the man and his works. *The New Grove Wagner* (Norton, 1984) contains an especially detailed catalog of Wagner's works and their sources; if John Deathridge's biographical section reads more like an errata list for previous literature than a coherent account in its own right, the survey of Wagner's musical and aesthetic achievements by Carl Dahlhaus is thoughtful and provocative. In the "Master Musicians" series, Barry Millington's *Wagner* (Vintage, 1987) offers a judiciously balanced account of both life and music, plus chronology, works list, personalia and bibliography.

In Wagner's massive and, for a long time, remarkably successful attempt to control posterity's view of him, his principal weapon was the autobiographical *My Life*, now available in a new translation by Andrew Gray, edited by Mary Whittall (Cambridge University Press, 1983). Not always true, but never less than enthralling, Wagner's account of his hard times and triumphs should be read with liberal dashes of salt (and Deathridge). An indispensable companion is the long-awaited *Selected Letters*, translated and edited by Stewart Spencer and Millington (Norton, 1988); representing perhaps 5 percent of Wagner's voluminous epistolary output, this well-chosen, well-annotated sampling includes crucial passages long suppressed. Wagner's image-building impulse pervades even the most personal documents, such as the diary he kept for Cosima (*The Diary of Richard Wagner: The Brown Book 1865–1882*, ed. Joachim Bergfeld, tr. George Bird; Cambridge, 1980) and Cosima's own diaries (*Cosima Wagner's Diaries*, ed. Martin Gregor-Dellin and Dietrich Mack, tr. Geoffrey Skelton; Harcourt Brace Jovanovich, 2 vols., 1978-80), but these also afford vivid, unguarded insights into Wagner's thought and intentions.

The classic biography is Ernest Newman's four-volume *The Life of Richard Wagner*, published between 1933 and 1947, now available in paperback (Cambridge), a work of enormous detail, narrative skill, erudition—and partisanship. Belonging to a generation still deeply divided over Wagner's significance, Newman concentrated on establishing the positive achievements. Modern scholarship has espoused a more detached view, to be found in the excellent recent biography by Martin Gregor-Dellin; deplorably, its translation by J. Maxwell Brownjohn,

Erich Leinsdorf, Vienna-born conductor for the four music dramas of Der Ring des Nibelungen *at the Metropolitan Opera, beginning with a debut* Die Walküre *in 1938 and concluding with performances of* Das Rheingold *and* Siegfried *in 1981*

Richard Wagner: His Life, His Work, His Century (Harcourt Brace Jovanovich, 1983), has been surreptitiously and savagely abridged. More than a mere coffee-table picture book is *Wagner: a Documentary Study*, edited by Herbert Barth, Dietrich Mack and Egon Voss (Oxford, 1975), including translated letters and documents as well as iconography.

For study of the operas themselves, the best starting point remains Newman's *The Wagner Operas* (Knopf, 1949), which emphasizes the sources of the librettos and explicates the dramatic action in greater detail than the musical structure. More broadly focused are the essays by Dahlhaus, *Richard Wagner's Music Dramas*, translated by Mary Whittall (Cambridge, 1979), devoted to the individual works and their cultural, theatrical and musical significance. *The Wagner Companion*, edited by Peter Burbidge and Richard Sutton (Cambridge, 1979), though somewhat of a mixed bag, includes valuable contributions on Wagner's musical background, language and compositional methods by (respectively) John Warrack, Deryck Cooke and Robert Bailey. Oswald Georg Bauer's *Richard Wagner: the Stage Designs and Productions from the Premieres to the Present* (Rizzoli, 1983) is a well-illustrated history of Wagner staging. Few of the provocative viewpoints on Wagner offered by modern German critics are available in English; one that is, Theodor Adorno's *In Search of Wagner*, translated by Rodney Livingstone (London: Verso, 1981), will be found both abrasive and stimulating.

From the beginning, the *Ring* has been a special subject of philosophical commentary. The most famous example is George Bernard Shaw's Socialist explication, *The Perfect Wagnerite*, first published in 1898 (paperback reprint, Dover, 1967); the brilliance of this encounter between two great intellects makes it still required reading. A more complex contemplation of the cycle was begun by the late Deryck Cooke. Sadly, *I Saw the World End: a Study of Wagner's "Ring"* (Oxford, 1979) represents but the first half (through *Die Walküre*) of the first half (the analysis of text and action) of the enormous work he contemplated, but even that much is full of insights to be pondered and debated. Robert Donington's *Wagner's "Ring" and its Symbols: the Music and the Myth* (St. Martin's, 1969) propounds a Jungian interpretation. Professedly more introductory in nature is John Culshaw's *Reflections on Wagner's "Ring"* (Viking, 1976), which originated as intermission talks for the Metropolitan Opera's *Ring* broadcasts of 1974-75. The excellent series of *Opera Guides* edited by Nicholas John for the English National Opera and the Royal Opera includes volumes on each of the *Ring* dramas (Riverrun Press, 1983-85), containing historical and musical essays, thematic guides and librettos—Andrew Porter's singing translations, which are also available in a single, typographically more attractive paperback (Norton, 1976). A fascinating footnote to the cycle's theatrical history is Heinrich Porges' *Wagner Rehearsing the "Ring,"* translated by Robert L. Jacobs (Cambridge, 1983), "an eye-witness account of the stage rehearsals of the first Bayreuth Festival."

David Hamilton has contributed articles on opera and music to numerous publications. He is the editor of The Metropolitan Opera Encyclopedia *and with Dorle J. Soria is co-producer of the Metropolitan Opera's Historic Broadcast Recordings.*

Götterdämmerung, as staged in the new production at the Metropolitan Opera: Right, Act I, Scene 2: disguised as Gunther through the magic of the Tarnhelm, Siegfried (Toni Krämer) wrests the Ring from Brünnhilde (Hildegard Behrens); Overleaf one, Act I, Scenes 1 and 2: in the hall of the Gibichungs, Hagen (Matti Salminen) meets with Gunther (Anthony Raffell) and Gutrune (Kathryn Harries) and, on the Valkyries' Rock, Waltraute (Christa Ludwig) tries to convince Brünnhilde (Hildegard Behrens) to relinquish the Ring to the Rhinemaidens; Overleaf two, Act II: outside the hall of the Gibichungs, Gutrune (Kathryn Harries) watches in horror as Brünnhilde (Hildegard Behrens), goaded by Hagen, accuses Siegfried (Toni Krämer) of deception—words that shock Gunther (Anthony Raffell)

GÖTTERDÄMMERUNG

Synopses of the Music Dramas

by Gerald Fitzgerald and John W. Freeman

DAS RHEINGOLD
(The Rhinegold)

Prologue in one act, four scenes
World premiere: Munich, Hofoper, September 22, 1869
U.S. premiere: New York, Metropolitan Opera, January 4, 1889

Cast of characters (in order of appearance)

Woglinde, *a Rhinemaiden, guardian of the river's gold* . . . . Soprano
Wellgunde, *a Rhinemaiden* . . . . Mezzo-soprano
Flosshilde, *a Rhinemaiden* . . . . Mezzo-soprano
Alberich, *a Nibelung blacksmith* . . . . Bass
Fricka, *goddess of marriage and morals* . . . . Mezzo-soprano
Wotan, *husband to Fricka, supreme god of the old order* . . . . Bass-baritone
Freia, *goddess of eternal youth, sister to Fricka* . . . . Soprano
Fasolt, *a giant* . . . . Bass
Fafner, *a giant, brother to Fasolt* . . . . Bass
Froh, *god of the fields and rain, brother to Fricka* . . . . Tenor
Donner, *god of thunder, wind and lightning, brother to Fricka* . . . . Baritone
Loge, *demigod of fire and mischief, kin to gods and Nibelungs* . . . . Tenor
Mime, *a Nibelung blacksmith, brother to Alberich* . . . . Tenor
Erda, *omniscient goddess of the earth* . . . . Contralto

In legendary times, Northern Europe consisted of three realms: the underworld, where the Nibelungs lived; the earth's surface, inhabited by giants and mortals; and the cloudy heights, home of the gods.

SCENE 1 (24 minutes): Deep under the Rhine, three of the river's daughters, custodians of a golden treasure, laugh while they play near an enormous rock, scarcely noticing when Alberich emerges from a crevice. Seized by desire, the sinister gnome tries to catch the nymphs as they dart through the waters, but his clumsy attempts lead to frustration. Taunts from his bewitching quarry merely quicken the Nibelung's lust and anger. Suddenly a gleam of sunlight illuminates the summit of the rock—the Rhinegold. Hailing the precious hoard, the nymphs are astonished that Alberich does not know what it represents. The Rhinegold is all-powerful, they tell him, and were it fashioned into a Ring, the wearer would rule the world. But the gold is safe, they continue, for whoever would steal the treasure must first renounce love. The Nibelung, aware his efforts at love yield only scorn, determines to seize the gold for himself, its power compensating any need for love. Scrambling up the rock, Alberich forswears love, wrests the prize free and escapes laughing. The waters are plunged in darkness as the Rhinemaidens, distraught over their loss, try to catch the thief.

SCENE 2 (48 minutes): As the sun rises over a mountainous plateau, Fricka and Wotan slumber on a bank of flowers. A fortress, their new home, gleams in the distance on a high cliff over the Rhine. When the two gods awaken, Wotan hails the building as a fulfillment of his dreams. Fricka, fearful for Freia, reproaches her husband for promising her sister to Fafner and Fasolt as payment for constructing the fortress. Wotan replies that he never seriously meant to keep the bargain. As the terrified Freia runs in, pursued by Fafner and Fasolt, Wotan says Loge will help the gods out of their dilemma. Now the giants

Das Rheingold, Scene 2: Wotan (James Morris) listens as Fricka (Waltraud Meier), fearful about Freia, expresses misgivings over the price promised for Valhalla

Götterdämmerung, as staged in the new production at the Metropolitan Opera: Overleaf, Act III, Scene 1: on the banks of the Rhine, Woglinde (Joyce Guyer), Flosshilde (Meredith Parsons) and Wellgunde (Diane Kesling) plead with Siegfried (Toni Krämer) to surrender the accursed Ring; Left, Act III, Scene 2: resolved to die on Siegfried's funeral pyre, Brünnhilde (Hildegard Behrens) prepares to throw herself into the flames, a selfless act that restores the Ring to the Rhinemaidens and thereby saves mankind

advance, armed with clubs, to claim their reward. When Wotan protests he made the pact in jest, that the giants must settle for another fee, Fasolt, smitten with Freia, balks. Fafner, intrigued that the loss of Freia's golden apples would cost the gods their eternal youth and therefore their power, decides the goddess must be taken by force. As the giants start to drag her away, Froh and Donner bar their path, Donner brandishing his hammer. Wotan intervenes, saying all treaties are guaranteed on his spear.

Loge, who originated the contract with the giants, and who at Wotan's command has been trying to find a suitable payment in lieu of Freia, materializes in a puff of smoke. Nothing in the world, he reports to the irate god, can replace woman's beauty, which only one creature—a Nibelung gnome—has forsworn in favor of power. The crafty fire god then relates how Alberich stole the Rhinegold, forging a Ring through which he can gain world dominance. Worried about Freia, Wotan at first dismisses the seemingly irrelevant tale, but the giants, fearing Alberich, show interest in the Rhinegold. When Fricka learns a wife could use the Ring to keep a philandering husband faithful, she urges Wotan to obtain it. Wotan is enthralled by the absolute power the Ring imparts. Since the Rhinemaidens want Wotan to restore the gold to them, proposes Loge, why not steal it, as Alberich did? Fafner, interested in the theft but lacking the guile to implement it, advises Wotan to use his wits to that purpose. Then, taking Freia hostage until evening, when the Nibelung's hoard must be delivered as ransom, the giants leave. No sooner does Freia disappear than a dense mist descends and the gods begin to weaken and age—the loss of Freia's golden apples, notes Loge, little changed because the goddess granted him fewer. Frightened, Fricka berates her husband for the shame she and the others bear. Wotan, now forced to a decision, bids Loge accompany him to the nether world to seek Alberich's treasure.

SCENE 3 (27 minutes): The clang of anvils pervades the dark caverns of Nibelheim, Alberich's underground domain, where he ceaselessly drives his slaves to mine gold to swell his hoard. Wearing the all-powerful Ring, the gnome torments Mime for the Tarnhelm he is fashioning. Mime, who covets this latest marvel for himself, must submit, and Alberich tries on the helmet, which transforms the wearer into any size or shape, protecting him from any foe. When the Tarnhelm enables Alberich to become invisible, he thrashes his defenseless brother, then vanishes to terrorize others he holds in bondage.

Das Rheingold, Scene 4: Alberich
(Franz Mazura), who has become lord of
the nether world, feels abject
humiliation when Wotan and Loge allow
his subjects, the Nibelungs, to
see him powerless—bound in a net, forced
to surrender his golden treasure

Soon a pair of visitors, Wotan and Loge, descend through a shaft before Mime, who complains of Alberich's tyranny, saying he had hoped to outwit his heartless brother by means of the Tarnhelm, regaining the Ring he forged for him. Unrecognized and amused by the complaining gnome, the gods offer to help the Nibelungs free themselves. Now Alberich returns, driving slaves who bear mounds of gold from his mines and who scurry away when he threatens them with the Ring. He knows Wotan and Loge and, though he need not fear them because of the Ring's power, he suspiciously questions their trip to Nibelheim. While sparring with them, he arrogantly warns of his plan to overthrow the gods and rule the world. Loge, choosing his words cleverly, asks the Nibelung what would happen if someone stole the Ring while he sleeps. How could they, the gnome asks, extolling the powers of the Tarnhelm. When Loge, feigning disbelief, asks for a demonstration, Alberich transforms himself into a large serpent, then back again. Loge asks whether the Tarnhelm can enable him to turn into something small—a toad, for instance —so he could hide. Obligingly, Alberich becomes a toad, whereupon Wotan traps the creature under his foot and Loge seizes the Tarnhelm from its head. As Alberich resumes his accustomed shape, he is tied and dragged by his captors to the surface of the earth.

SCENE 4 (55 minutes): Once more on the plateau, Loge and Wotan inform their prisoner he cannot go free without forfeiting his hoard as ransom. Outraged at the demand, he acquiesces, certain that through the Ring he can replenish his fortune. Loge unties his right hand, enabling Alberich to kiss the Ring to summon his slaves, who haul up the gold they have mined, piling it in a heap before returning, with shrieks of fear, to Nibelheim. The gods' command obeyed, he asks for the return of the Tarnhelm, but Loge says the gods will keep it. Wotan adds that the Ring also must be part of the booty, reminding the gnome that from the start it was not rightfully his. Alberich retorts that Wotan is as much a thief as he, but this does not prevent the god from tearing the Ring from his finger. Loge unfastens the Nibelung's bonds, saying he may go. The embittered gnome greets his freedom by hurling forth a curse on the Ring: until it returns to his hand, may care, envy and death befall all who possess it.

Alberich disappears as the other gods approach, followed by the giants with their hostage, Freia. Saddened at losing the goddess, Fasolt agrees to accept the Nibelung hoard only if it hides her from his view. The brothers thrust their clubs into the ground to support the treasure, which Loge and Froh heap up in front of Freia. Fasolt complains that the gold is not quite enough—he can still see Freia's hair through a crack—forcing Loge reluctantly to add the Tarnhelm to the hoard. Then Fasolt complains he can see the gleam of Freia's eye through a chink. At this Fafner commands Wotan to close the gap with the Ring, now gleaming on his finger. When Wotan vehemently refuses, the giants pull Freia from behind the hoard to abduct her. But darkness suddenly covers the mountaintop as a deep cleft in the ground opens and Erda materializes, roused from perpetual sleep by the conflict. The earth goddess warns Wotan to yield the Ring, which spells doom for the gods. Though he would know more, Erda disappears. Persuaded by her counsel, Wotan tosses the Ring onto the hoard, whereupon the grateful Freia is released and the giants begin packing their payment into a sack. At once Alberich's curse takes effect: the brothers quarrel over how to divide the spoils. Loge slyly advises Fasolt to keep the Ring and let Fafner take everything else. When the giants struggle over the Ring, Fafner brutally kills Fasolt, claiming Ring, Tarnhelm and hoard for himself.

After he has gone, Fricka bids Wotan turn his thoughts to their new home. Donner, swinging his hammer, summons lightning and thunder to dispel thick mists that have enveloped the mountaintop. As the heavens clear, a rainbow forms a bridge to the fortress. Noting how the setting sun gilds the noble structure, Wotan tells Fricka their abode is called Valhalla. While Wotan leads the gods across the rainbow, Loge muses that they are headed toward their downfall, confessing he would like to consume them all. From below, the Rhinemaidens, heard grieving for their lost treasure, disturb the gods' passage but draw no sympathy. The nymphs' song has an ominous note: truth and purity lie only in the depths, the gods are false and weak.

Das Rheingold, Scene 4: great bundles of gold are stacked in front of Freia (Ellen Shade) to hide the goddess from the sight of Wotan's creditors, Fasolt and Fafner, who have accepted Alberich's riches as the fee for building Valhalla

DIE WALKÜRE

(The Valkyrie)

Music Drama in three acts
World premiere: Munich, Hofoper, June 26, 1870
U.S. premiere: New York, Metropolitan Opera, January 30, 1885

Cast of characters (in order of appearance)

Siegmund, *a Wälsung, mortal son of Wotan by a she-wolf* . . . . Tenor
Sieglinde, *his twin sister* . . . . Soprano
Hunding, *husband of Sieglinde, a tribal chieftain* . . . . Bass
Brünnhilde, *a Valkyrie, warrior daughter of Wotan and Erda* . . . . Soprano
Wotan, *supreme god of the old order* . . . . Bass-baritone
Fricka, *his wife, goddess of marriage and morals* . . . . Mezzo-soprano
Gerhilde, *a Valkyrie, another of Wotan's warrior daughters* . . . . Soprano
Helmwige, *a Valkyrie* . . . . Soprano
Waltraute, *a Valkyrie* . . . . Mezzo-soprano
Schwertleite, *a Valkyrie* . . . . Mezzo-soprano
Ortlinde, *a Valkyrie* . . . . Soprano
Siegrune, *a Valkyrie* . . . . Mezzo-soprano
Grimgerde, *a Valkyrie* . . . . Mezzo-soprano
Rossweisse, *a Valkyrie* . . . . Mezzo-soprano

Many years after the events of *Das Rheingold*, the Nibelung treasure, including the Ring, remains in the clutches of Fafner. The giant has used the Tarnhelm to transform himself into a dragon in order to guard the ill-gotten hoard, which he has stored in a cave deep in the forest. The curse is dormant, for Fafner sleeps most of the time. Living as a mortal near Fafner's lair, Wotan with a she-wolf sires twins, Siegmund and Sieglinde—first of a race of heroes, the Wälsungs, through which Wotan hopes to restore the Ring to the Rhinemaidens, freeing the gods at last from Alberich's curse. To accomplish this scheme, Wotan allows the twins to be separated during early childhood, then abandons his son — for the Wälsungs must act as free agents to recover the Ring. Only after years of travail and suffering are Siegmund and Sieglinde reunited — and when they meet, they do not recognize each other.

Die Walküre, Act I: Hunding (Aage Haugland), while sharing supper with a stranger who has entered his house, discovers that he is in fact sheltering an enemy

ACT I (65 minutes): A primitive dwelling built around the trunk of a great ash tree in the forests of northern Europe. As a storm rages, Siegmund, a stranger to the place, stumbles through the door and collapses in exhaustion on a bear rug near an open fire. There the wounded youth is discovered by Sieglinde, wife of the house, who fetches water when he cries out in thirst. The two are attracted to each other at once. Thanking her, the youth learns she is married to Hunding, and that he is welcome to remain until her husband returns from the hunt. Siegmund reassures her he poses no threat: disarmed by foes, he barely escaped with his life. Sieglinde offers him a horn of nourishing honeyed mead, and they look with curious longing into each other's eyes. When Siegfried, mindful of his persistent ill luck, abruptly states he must leave, she entreats him to remain, for he can bring no unhappiness to a home where unhappiness already abides. He will stay, he says, since his name is Wehwalt (one ruled by woe).

The sound of horses and the slamming of a stable door are heard, and Hunding enters, armed with shield and spear. Scowling, he scrutinizes his unexpected guest with mistrust but declares the sacred hospitality of his hearth. After ordering Sieglinde to prepare food, Hunding notices Siegmund's uncanny resemblance to his wife. When he asks the stranger who is, Siegmund once more identifies himself as Wehwalt. One day, he relates, when only a child, he came home from hunting with his father, Wolfe, to find his mother killed, their home laid waste and his twin sister missing. The Neidings, his father's enemies, had done this. Hunding comments he has heard tales of Wolfe and his cub. The story continues with Siegmund's years of wandering in the wild and the disappearance of his father during a skirmish with the Neidings. Only one trace of the parent was found by the son — a wolfskin. After this, though he tried to establish a new home, every clan treated him as an outcast. His most recent adventure involved the attempted rescue of a girl from a forced wedding. Protecting her, he killed her brothers, but because the grieving bride would not leave them, she died at the hands of angry tribesmen, and Siegmund himself was wounded. Hunding angrily proclaims that he, summoned to this very conflict, arrived after the bloodshed, and that it was his own clansmen Siegmund had slaughtered. Stonily, he says that ancient custom requires him to offer any wayfarer shelter for the night, but the next morning he and Siegmund must fight to the death. Grasping his weapons, Hunding goes to bed, brusquely instructing Sieglinde to prepare his nightly drink. As the frightened woman takes the draught to him, she looks searchingly at the stranger, then directs her eyes toward a spot on the ash tree.

When Siegmund is alone, the weaponless youth recalls that his father promised him a sword in time of need. In desperation he calls on his parent, whom he now addresses as Wälse. Seemingly in answer, a ray of light from the fire illuminates a metal object shining in the tree trunk, momentarily catching Siegmund's attention. As he muses on the kind woman who has helped him, Sieglinde steals back into the room, urging him to flee, saying she has drugged Hunding with a sleeping potion. Then she describes an extraordinary event that took place at the time she was compelled to marry Hunding: during the wedding feast, an aged man (Wotan, disguised as the Wanderer) appeared among the fearful guests, thrusting a sword deep into the trunk of the ash tree. Ever since, the weapon has resisted all efforts to wrest it forth, and the sword still remains a challenge to whoever can extract it. Impulsively, Siegmund cries he shall claim the blade as his own. As the two embrace, the door is flung open by a gust of wind, startling Sieglinde. The forest, bathed in spring moonlight, is revealed, and to calm Sieglinde's apprehension, Siegfried describes spring and love as brother and sister, saying one sets the other free. Ecstatically she responds that he is the spring for which she has yearned, come to free her from the long cold of winter. Looking into his eyes, she notes that his face reflects her own just as surely as the brook. When he reveals that his father, known as Wolfe to cowards, was really Wälse, she is beside herself with excitement, realizing the stranger is a Wälsung — in fact, her long-lost twin brother. Now it is clear that the sword was thrust into the tree for Siegmund. Grasping the hilt of the weapon, which he names Nothung

(Needful), the youth draws forth the gleaming blade. With a shriek of joy, Sieglinde pronounces herself the prize won by Siegmund with the sword. Claiming his sister as bride, he runs with her into the night.

ACT II (95 minutes): In a mountain gorge, Wotan tells his Valkyrie daughter Brünnhilde to bridle her horse for a dispute in which she will defend Siegmund from Hunding, who is now pursuing the lovers through the forest. The girl cries out in excitement at the prospect of combat but, seeing Fricka approach in a ram-drawn chariot, warns the god of impending marital strife.

As the warrior maiden disappears among the rocks, the irate goddess of hearth and home confronts Wotan on behalf of Hunding's marriage rights. Wotan claims that compulsory, loveless vows are not sacred, but Fricka points out the Wälsung twins are guilty not only of adultery but of incest. When the god asks that she bless the union, Fricka scoffs, saying that in begetting the Wälsungs and the Valkyries Wotan himself made a mockery of marriage, debasing all the gods. Siegmund is no free agent, she continues, but merely Wotan's tool—and, out of respect for her honor, he must die. Further, during the fight with Hunding, Wotan must remove the sword's magic power and prevent Brünnhilde's intervention. Worn down by his wife's tirade, Wotan betrays by his expression that he will bow to her demands.

Brünnhilde returns as Fricka, her mission accomplished, rides away. In shame and frustration, Wotan turns to the Valkyrie to pour out his heart, relating how he made off with Alberich's golden treasure to pay for Valhalla, and how Erda warned him of the Ring's evil power. After that, he descended into the earth to learn more from Erda and became her lover, begetting Brünnhilde and her eight sister Valkyries. With their help, he hoped to stem the tide of the gods' decline by building an army of mighty warriors. Erda had warned that if Alberich regained the Ring, he would destroy the gods. The giant Fafner, Valhalla's surviving builder, now guards the treasure, and Wotan cannot reclaim it by his own actions, so he needs a hero to do this for him—someone outside his own control, unaided by his power. Siegmund is such a hero, but now Fricka demands his death. Tainted by contact with the Ring, Wotan bitterly observes, he must renounce whatever he loves, betray whoever trusts him and wait in resignation for the end. Lately he has learned that Alberich bought himself a wife and produced a son, born of hate, who will fulfill Erda's prophecy by causing the gods' ruin. Revoking his previous orders, Wotan tells Brünnhilde she must do what Fricka asks: Siegmund must die. Seeing her father set against himself, the Valkyrie argues she must save Siegmund because Wotan loves him. But the god warns her of his wrath if she disobeys, then storms off, leaving her saddened and confused.

Die Walküre, Act I: Siegmund (Gary Lakes) seizes the handle of the sword Nothung left for him by his father, wresting it from the trunk of the great ash tree

She withdraws as the Wälsungs approach. Siegmund bids Sieglinde rest, for she is near collapse. Seized by guilt, the girl imagines Hunding's pursuit and Siegmund's defeat. When she sinks to the ground in exhaustion, Siegmund kisses her brow, keeping watch as she rests. Brünnhilde appears on the mountainside to warn him of death, saying that soon, like other fallen heroes, he will enter Valhalla. When he learns that Sieglinde cannot accompany him to Wotan's fortress, he refuses. Brünnhilde insists he must die, that his sword has lost its magic power. At these words Siegmund sadly contemplates the sleeping Sieglinde, lamenting the cruel destiny they share. Moved by the depth of his love, Brünnhilde decides to ignore Wotan's command. She promises to protect the Wälsung from Hunding, then vanishes. Soon the enemy is heard approaching. When the fitfully sleeping Sieglinde wakes, she discovers Siegmund and Hunding engaged in deadly combat. Wotan suddenly appears and, waving Brünnhilde aside as she shields Siegmund, shatters the magic sword with his spear, permitting Hunding to kill his foe. The horrified Valkyrie, gathering up the broken remnants of Nothung, escapes with Sieglinde to avoid Wotan's ire. Grief-stricken by the death of his valiant son, Wotan fells Hunding with a contemptuous glare. Then, furious over Brünnhilde's disobedience, he sets out after her.

ACT III (70 minutes): The Valkyries ride their steeds through the heavens, bearing the bodies of slain heroes to Valhalla. As they gather high on a mountaintop, they see Brünnhilde riding hard in their direction, growing alarmed as they realize she carries not a hero but a woman across her saddle. Brünnhilde dismounts and rushes onto the height with Sieglinde, breathlessly explaining all that has happened, pleading with her sisters for a fresh horse. In the distance, surrounded by a threatening cloud, Wotan is spotted approaching, which makes the Valkyries hesitate to help Brünnhilde and the Wälsung. Sieglinde revives, numb with despair, asking only for death. When Brünnhilde tells her

Die Walküre, Act III: pleading that a
blazing barrier protect the
Valkyries' Rock while she sleeps,
Brünnhilde (Hildegard Behrens) falls into the
arms of Wotan (Simon Estes),
knowing he will grant her final wish

she must live, for she will give birth to Siegmund's child, the woman cries out in hope, begging to be saved. Offering advice, the other Valkyries note that Wotan avoids a forest to the east, where Fafner guards the Nibelung treasure. Brünnhilde urges Sieglinde to flee there while she herself remains behind to bear the brunt of Wotan's anger, going on to predict that the woman's unborn child will be the hero Siegfried. Sieglinde, gratefully clutching fragments of Siegmund's sword, hastens away.

When Wotan rages onto the rock, searching for Brünnhilde, the Valkyries try to hide their sister, but it is not long before she steps forward to learn her punishment. By disobeying, Wotan declares, she has chosen her own fate: banishment. Cut off from duties and privileges as a Valkyrie, no longer one of the gods, she is condemned to sleep on the Valkyries' Rock, prey to the first mortal man who finds her. Crying out in terror at the harshness of his decision, the other Valkyries gallop away amid lightning and thunder.

As evening falls and the heavens clear, Brünnhilde remains on the mountaintop with her father, whose anger has slowly abated. Kneeling before him, she asks if what she did was so shameful. In protecting his favored children, she was true to his inner wishes rather than his outward pronouncements, words exacted by Fricka. Had he but seen the need in Siegmund's eyes.... Wotan seems unmoved, replying that just as he shunned his impulse to save Siegmund, he now must shun Brünnhilde. The Valkyrie counters that in casting her off he mocks his own honor. The god retorts that in yielding to love she has condemned herself to live as a mortal. When Brünnhilde reminds him of the child to be born to Sieglinde, Wotan furiously exclaims he has renounced the Wälsungs, and that is that. Realizing she has lost, Brünnhilde asks again about her destiny. Wotan repeats she will lie in sleep on the Valkyrie Rock, prize to the first man who finds her. Fervently the Valkyrie pleads for at least one grace: while she sleeps, let fire surround the rock, assurance that only a hero will penetrate the flames. Overcome with emotion, Wotan takes his daughter in his arms, bidding her a tender farewell. Then he kisses her eyes to end her godhood, whereupon she falls into deep slumber. Striking his spear on a rock, he summons Loge to build a wall of Magic Fire around the mountaintop, decreeing that only a hero unafraid of his spear's point shall brave the flames to awaken the sleeping maiden. Overcome with sadness and resignation, he disappears.

SIEGFRIED

Music Drama in three acts, four scenes
World premiere: Bayreuth, Festspielhaus, August 16, 1876
U.S. premiere: New York, Metropolitan Opera, November 9, 1887

Cast of characters (in order of appearance)
Mime, a Nibelung . . . . Tenor
Siegfried, son of Siegmund and Sieglinde, reared by Mime . . . . Tenor
Wanderer, the disguised king of the gods, Wotan . . . . Bass-baritone
Alberich, former king of the Nibelungs, brother of Mime . . . . Bass
Fafner, a giant transformed into a dragon . . . . Bass
Forest Bird . . . . Soprano
Erda, omniscient goddess of the earth . . . . Contralto
Brünnhilde, a banished Valkyrie, daughter of Erda and Wotan . . . . Soprano

Two decades following the action of Die Walküre, Fafner the giant remains transformed into a dragon by the Tarnhelm, guarding the Ring and the rest of the Nibelung treasure in a cave deep in the forest. Sieglinde, after giving birth to a son, has died in the same forest, where she managed to elude Wotan, finding shelter with Mime in his smithy. Ever since, the Nibelung has taken charge of the child, realizing that he will grow into a hero capable of retrieving the Nibelung hoard from Fafner. Meanwhile, Brünnhilde sleeps on the mountaintop, protected by Magic Fire. Only a man undaunted by Wotan's spear, symbol of the gods' power, can brave the flames to awaken her.

ACT I (83 minutes): In his cavern workshop, near Fafner's lair, Mime complains bitterly as he toils at an anvil in an attempt to forge a new sword for Siegfried, who has grown to manhood. The impotent, hate-filled Nibelung has fashioned many previous blades for his ward, but when the exuberant youth tested them, they always broke into pieces. Though Mime secretly has kept the shattered Nothung, the magic sword wielded by Siegfried's father, he lacks the skill to restore its fragments. If he could do so, with Siegfried's help, he would fulfill his dream of obtaining Fafner's Ring and becoming ruler of the world. A hunting horn announces the approach of Siegfried, who bounds in with a bear he has captured, playfully scaring Mime before releasing the animal to the forest. Impatient for a new sword, Siegfried grasps Mime's latest effort, only to have the weapon snap like a toy in his hands. To avoid the headstrong youth's anger, the Nibelung offers him kind words and food, both brusquely rebuffed. At this, Mime whiningly reminds Siegfried of the long years he has looked after him and all he has taught him. Siegfried replies he has never learned to tolerate the sight of Mime, nor does he understand why he always returns to his workshop. They do not resemble each other, he notes, grabbing Mime by the throat with the demand to know who his real parents were. Under threat, the Nibelung confesses the truth: years ago he found a woman in distress in the woods and nursed her as she died giving birth. Her name was Sieglinde, and the baby's father had fallen in combat; Siegfried's name is a legacy from his mother. Moved by the story, Siegfried asks for proof of what he has been told, at which Mime takes forth the splintered remnants of the sword Nothung. At once the youth insists the weapon be welded whole so that he can go forth into the world to seek adventure, leaving Mime forever. As Siegfried runs back into the forest, the frustrated gnome moans he will never be able to fix the sword.

As he sits dejected, an aged Wanderer garbed in a long cloak and broad-brimmed hat appears, weary from his travels, seeking hospitality. Soon the insistent and unwanted guest suggests a battle of wits in which he will forfeit his head should he lose. Mime, though suspicious, agrees, then proceeds to ask the Wanderer three questions: what race lives under the earth (the Nibelungs), on the face of the earth (the giants) and on the cloudy heights (the gods)? Not only does the Wanderer answer correctly, but he describes Alberich's cursed Ring, Fafner's guardianship of the treasure and the origins of Wotan's powerful spear, which he strikes on the ground for emphasis, terrifying Mime, who recognizes the identity of his mysterious guest. Now the Wanderer demands that Mime too answer three questions, with the Nibelung's head the price of failure. What is the race Wotan mistreats but loves most? Mime correctly names the Wälsungs. What is the sword Siegfried must use if he is to kill the dragon Fafner? Nothung, says Mime. And who will repair the sword? When Mime cannot respond, the Wanderer tells him the sword can be forged only by one who has never known fear—and he leaves Mime's head as bounty to that person. The visitor departs in peace, but the Nibelung is totally unnerved by their encounter.

Hearing distant growls, Mime panics, thinking Fafner is coming, but it is only Siegfried, anxious to wield his father's sword. Mime, worried for his life, tries to find out whether the youth comprehends the meaning of fear. Since he does not, Mime decides to take him to Fafner's lair, where he will surely learn. When Siegfried once more orders Mime to finish Nothung, the Nibelung sobs that he lacks the craft, at which Siegfried decides to repair the sword himself, launching into a spirited forging song as he works. While the youth toils at his task, Mime plots to get rid of him: once the dragon has been slain and the treasure recovered, Mime will give the tired hero a sleeping potion, then kill him with his own weapon. Siegfried, shredding and melting the metal, pours it into a mold, next placing the newly cast blade on the anvil to hammer it into final shape. As he tempers the finished steel in water, Mime shares his elation, imagining how he will turn the tables on his detested brother Alberich. Siegfried brandishes the magic sword, splits the anvil with it and dashes off into the forest.

ACT II (79 minutes): That night, Alberich keeps vigil near Fafner's cave, brooding over his lost treasure, determined to regain the Ring. The Wanderer approaches, bathed in an eerie light, and the Nibelung at once recognizes him as Wotan. Though Alberich heaps recriminations upon the god, reminding him he cannot steal the Ring from Fafner,

Siegfried, Act I: Mime (Horst Hiestermann), clutching the remnants of Nothung, despairs that his skills as smithy are deficient to reforge the weapon for Siegfried and thereby regain the all-powerful Ring

Siegfried, Act II: in the forest, hoping
to encounter Fafner the dragon,
Siegfried (Wolfgang Neumann) fashions a reed
pipe to imitate a benevolent Forest Bird

the Wanderer replies that he no longer cares about the Ring—he is now only an observer of destiny. He adds that it is Mime whom Alberich should fear, for Mime wants the gold and now brings a valiant young hero to slay Fafner. The Nibelung is perplexed that the king of the gods, his enemy, seems to be helping him. Wotan and Alberich rouse the sleeping Fafner to warn him of approaching danger, urging him to surrender the Ring to save his life. Fafner mumbles he will devour any attacker. Once more, the Wanderer warns Alberich about Mime. Then god and Nibelung disappear in the shadows.

As dawn breaks, sunlight penetrates the dense foliage of the forest. Mime enters with Siegfried, showing him Fafner's lair—the place where Siegfried hopes to learn what fear means. Dismissed by the youth, the treacherous gnome hobbles off, muttering that he hopes Siegfried and Fafner kill each other. Siegfried stretches on the ground under a lime tree to rest, enchanted by the murmur of the forest, yearning for the mother he never knew. A Forest Bird, high in the branches over his head, keeps him company, warbling a song he wishes he could understand. Cutting a reed and blowing on it, Siegfried tries to imitate the bird; but his effort is pinched and sour. Then he raises his silver hunting horn to his lips, hoping to attract some other friend with its fanfare. Inadvertently he awakens Fafner, who rumbles forth from his den. During the struggle that ensues, Siegfried plunges his magic sword into the monster's heart. Dying, Fafner warns the youth that whoever instigated their fight is plotting his death as well. When Siegfried draws Nothung from the beast, his fingers are burned by blood, and, to cool them, he touches them to his lips. The taste of the dragon's blood gives him the power to understand the language of the Forest Bird, who tells him of the Nibelung hoard, the Tarnhelm and the all-powerful Ring. No sooner does Siegfried disappear into the cave to inspect the treasure than Mime slinks back, only to confront Alberich, who tries to bar his path. The brothers quarrel over the spoils, withdrawing when Siegfried reappears carrying proof of his victory—the Tarnhelm, which he fastens to his belt, and the Ring, which he places on his hand. Now the Forest Bird warns Siegfried about Mime, saying the taste of dragon's blood will enable him to read the gnome's thoughts. Soon Mime creeps forward, bearing the drugged drink, wondering if he has learned fear. Despite his solicitous words, Siegfried understands his intentions—to trick and destroy him, then to seize the treasure. Offered the drink, the youth loses patience with the Nibelung and kills him, whereupon Alberich's mocking laughter echoes in the distance. Siegfried places Mime's body in the cave with the treasure he so desired, then uses Fafner's corpse to seal the entrance. While he rests, lamenting his solitude, longing for a loving companion, he calls on the Forest Bird for advice. To his delight, the bird tells him of a wondrous maiden who rests on a fire-encircled rock—Brünnhilde, a bride who can be won only by a hero who knows no fear. Siegfried exclaims he has yet to learn fear, hoping that Brünnhilde can teach it to him. Enthralled, the young hero runs through the forest toward the mountain where she sleeps, the Forest Bird guiding his way.

ACT III, SCENE 1 (31 minutes): By night, as thunder and lightning threaten a wild mountain gorge, the Wanderer summons Erda from sleep deep in a cave. Concealing his identity, he seeks knowledge of the future. Erda evades the questions, saying he should consult the Norns, who weave the Rope of Destiny, or Brünnhilde. Then he demands to know how he can alter the fate of the gods. At this, Erda recognizes him and cries out in apprehension. The Wanderer, resigning himself to Valhalla's doom, bequeaths the world to the redemptive power of Brünnhilde's love. He commands Erda to go back into the earth, where she will find eternal rest: her wisdom is needed no longer.

Siegfried ventures into the gorge, preceded by the Forest Bird, seeking Brünnhilde's rock. The Wanderer is pleased to encounter his grandson, inquiring with humor about his exploits and the sword he wears. But Siegfried, eager to reach his goal, responds arrogantly, angering the god, who tries to block his path. Drawing Nothung, the youth splinters the Wanderer's spear with a single stroke. Realizing his power has ended, the stunned deity retrieves the broken pieces of the mighty weapon, which once shattered Nothung. The Wanderer vanishes as Siegfried scales the mountain to penetrate the Magic Fire.

SCENE 2 (52 minutes): Dawn breaks bright on the rocky height where Brünnhilde rests. Reaching the summit, Siegfried discovers an armed, sleeping figure, which he assumes to be a man. When he removes the Valkyrie's shield, helmet and breastplate, however, he finds instead the first woman he has ever seen. Finally sensing fear, he invokes the spirit of his mother in his distress. Unsure of how to awaken the maiden, and overcome by her beauty, he summons the courage to kiss her lips. Brünnhilde, roused from long slumber, begins to stir, and when she slowly realizes she is not dreaming, that Siegfried has come, she hails the sunlight and her return to life. As she tells the hero she loved him even before he was born, he momentarily mistakes her for his mother. The banished Valkyrie speaks of his parents and her own role in their last moments on earth, but her words only further confuse him. Unfamiliar emotions alarm Siegfried, and Brünnhilde too feels strange. She sees her horse Grane grazing nearby, and kneels to hold the weapons that were once her protection. When Siegfried tries to embrace her, she starts in alarm: no god ever dared touch her. Forgetting Wotan has ended her godhood, she protests that earthly passion would destroy her immortality. But she *is* mortal, no longer a Valkyrie, and womanly ardor soon replaces all shame and fear. Joyously throwing herself into Siegfried's arms, she bids farewell to memories of Valhalla, abandoning herself to human love, exulting even in thoughts of death.

GÖTTERDÄMMERUNG
(Twilight of the Gods)

Music Drama in prologue and three acts, six scenes
World premiere: Bayreuth, Festspielhaus, August 17, 1876
U.S. premiere: New York, Metropolitan Opera, January 25, 1888

Cast of characters (in order of appearance)
First Norn, *a goddess of fate, Erda's daughter* . . . . Contralto
Second Norn, *a goddess of fate* . . . . Mezzo-soprano
Third Norn, *a goddess of fate* . . . . Soprano
Brünnhilde, *now a mortal, daughter of Erda and Wotan* . . . . Soprano
Siegfried, *a hero, son of Siegmund and Sieglinde* . . . . Tenor
Gunther, *king of the Gibichungs, son of Gibich and Grimhild* . . . . Baritone
Hagen, *his half brother, son of Alberich and Grimhild* . . . . Bass
Gutrune, *Gunther's sister* . . . . Soprano
Waltraute, *a Valkyrie* . . . . Mezzo-soprano
Alberich, *a Nibelung* . . . . Bass
Woglinde, *a Rhinemaiden* . . . . Soprano
Wellgunde, *a Rhinemaiden* . . . . Mezzo-soprano
Flosshilde, *a Rhinemaiden* . . . . Mezzo-soprano
First Vassal, *a Gibichung* . . . . Tenor
Second Vassal, *a Gibichung* . . . . Baritone

Götterdämmerung, Prologue: Siegfried (Toni Krämer) and his bride, Brünnhilde (Hildegard Behrens), bid one another an exuberant farewell as the hero prepares to seek adventure along the Rhine

Following their meeting in *Siegfried*, Brünnhilde and Siegfried live together for a time in their remote mountain abode. Unknown to them, danger lurks in the valley below their rocky heights: Alberich, having lost his treasure and power, schemes to regain both. Though he renounced love when he seized the Rhinegold from the Rhinemaidens, he sired a son, "born of hate," by bribing Grimhild, a woman of a Rhineland tribe, to submit to him. This son, Hagen, now grown to maturity, waits for the chance to further the Nibelung's aims, hoping to be his eventual heir.

PROLOGUE (38 minutes): At night on the Valkyries' rock, while Siegfried and Brünnhilde sleep in a cave, the Norns weave the earth mother Erda's wisdom into the Rope of Destiny. These baleful goddesses, mindful of man's suffering and the perfidy of the gods, recall how the world ash tree, once flourishing and the source of Wotan's spear, has been broken into pieces and placed around Valhalla, his fortress. The shattered remnants of the tree form a funeral pyre that will be ignited by Loge, god of fire, when the old order must perish. Suddenly, at the mention of Alberich and his theft of the Rhinegold, the skein the Norns are weaving breaks, signifying an end to their task. Terrified, the three veiled figures descend into the earth to seek Erda.

At dawn, Siegfried and Brünnhilde emerge from the cave, exultant in their newfound union. The former Valkyrie, having given the hero her armor and taught him all she knows, sends him forth to new deeds of valor, recounting how he fearlessly killed the dragon Fafner and climbed the fire-encircled mountain to awaken her to life as a mortal. Siegfried, to remind her of his devotion, gives Brünnhilde the magic Ring he took from the dragon, and she offers him her horse Grane in exchange. Rapturously they bid each other farewell before the hero begins a journey down the Rhine. Brünnhilde waves to her beloved as his horn resounds in the valley below.

ACT I, SCENE 1 (42 minutes): In the gloomy hall of the Gibichungs, a fierce and warlike river tribe, Gunther and Gutrune take council from Hagen concerning the royal fortunes, which have waned. While Hagen envies the cowardly, vacillating Gunther his legitimacy, Gunther covets his half brother's fierceness and cunning. Hagen advises Gunther and Gutrune to strengthen their rule through marriage, suggesting Brünnhilde, the fire-girded Valkyrie, as Gunther's bride and Siegfried, the mighty warrior, as Gutrune's husband. Through a ruse, Hagen continues, a daring scheme is possible: a magic potion of forgetfulness will make Siegfried fall in love with Gutrune, and to obtain her as his wife, he will win Brünnhilde for Gunther. In fact, Hagen is hatching a plot to claim his birthright as Alberich's son—the all-powerful Ring and Tarnhelm, which, once in his possession, will make him ruler of the world.

A horn call announces Siegfried's approach, and Hagen, sighting him in a boat, hails him ashore. Following exchanges of greeting, Siegfried speaks of his exploits, and of a woman who now wears the Ring he took from a dragon. Hagen tells the hero about the enchanted powers of the Tarnhelm, fastened to his belt; then Gutrune steps forward to give Siegfried the potion, which causes him to lose all memory of Brünnhilde and urgently seek marriage to Gutrune. Now Gunther describes an unattainable bride he himself desires—a maiden on a fiery mountaintop—and Siegfried offers to brave the flames to win her for Gunther, using the Tarnhelm to transform himself into Gunther's likeness to deceive the woman until he can deliver her to the king. Gunther and Siegfried take an oath of blood brotherhood, but Hagen declines to join the pledge, declaring his own blood cold and sluggish. After the two men depart in the boat, Hagen keeps vigil on the banks of the Rhine, consumed with desire for the Ring.

SCENE 2 (39 minutes): On the mountaintop, as Brünnhilde waits for Siegfried to return, she tenderly kisses the Ring. Her revery is disturbed by lightning and thunder, heralding the unexpected arrival of a sister Valkyrie, Waltraute. Impelled by the decline of Valhalla, Waltraute has left the fortress, risking Wotan's wrath, to implore Brünnhilde's aid in saving the gods. The only remedy for their impending doom, she says in agitation, is for Brünnhilde to surrender the Ring to the Rhinemaidens, thereby lifting Alberich's curse. Shocked by the request, Brünnhilde refuses, declaring Siegfried's love more important than the gods' fate. Waltraute rushes away in despair. As storm clouds gather and the flames around the mountain peak begin to blaze anew, Siegfried's horn sounds in the distance. But Brünnhilde's joy turns to confusion and fear when a strange, ominous figure steps before her, claiming her as bride in Gunther's name and violently wresting the Ring from her hand. In shame the vanquished woman enters the cave. Siegfried draws his sword as witness that his promise to Gunther will be honorably kept; then he too enters the cave.

ACT II (66 minutes): In the dark of night, while Hagen sleeps outside the Gibichung hall, Alberich appears as if in a dream, extracting from his son the pledge he will defeat Siegfried and regain the Ring. The gnome vanishes with the dawn.

Siegfried, transported by the magic of the Tarnhelm, arrives on the shore, cheerfully describing his successful quest to Hagen and Gutrune. Gunther and Brünnhilde will soon follow by boat, he says. A sail is sighted, and when Hagen sounds his oxhorn, summoning the Gibichung clan to greet their king, other horns powerfully answer from the surrounding area. As the vassals congregate, Hagen tells them weapons will be needed only to prepare sacrifices for a wedding feast, instructing them to welcome Gunther's bride and to avenge any wrong, should one have been committed. When Brünnhilde is proudly led before the assembly by Gunther, the vassals noisily strike their weapons against their shields in homage. Then the dazed, humiliated woman sees Siegfried, and after falling back astonished, she flies into a rage. He, still under the spell of the potion, innocently tells her that he is to marry Gutrune and that she will become Gunther's wife. Spying the Ring on Siegfried's finger, Brünnhilde demands to know how he obtained it,

Götterdämmerung, Act I: Gunther (Anthony Raffell), chief of the Gibichungs, with his sister, Gutrune (Kathryn Harries), who are tricked by their half brother, Hagen, into seeking alliances with Brünnhilde and Siegfried

since only the night before it had been ripped from her hand by Gunther. Hagen fans the flames of the argument, telling Brünnhilde to be more specific. Charging Siegfried with theft of the Ring, she declares *he* is her husband, that he forced himself upon her. The vassals clamor to protect Gunther's honor as Siegfried protests, swearing on a spear, proffered by Hagen, that he has not lied or done any wrong, recalling only that he took the Ring from a dragon. Brünnhilde, grasping the spear, furiously shouts that for his treachery Siegfried should die by this very weapon. Siegfried tries to dismiss her accusations and invites the vassals to celebrate, leading Gutrune into the hall.

Brünnhilde, baffled by all that has transpired, is torn by fury and anguish. When she cries out for vengeance, Hagen offers to kill Siegfried. Brünnhilde sarcastically laughs, telling him the hero is invincible—that she has protected him with magic, except for his back, which he would never turn to a foe. There I will strike, retorts Hagen. At first, Gunther is hesitant about the murder, partly because of Gutrune's happiness, partly because of the oath of brotherhood he took with Siegfried. Taunted by Brünnhilde and lured by Hagen's description of the Ring's power, Gunther in the end agrees that Siegfried must die. Hagen suggests the crime take place the next day during a hunting expedition. While Gunther and Brünnhilde implore the gods for assistance, Hagen invokes Alberich. Then the wedding procession of Siegfried and Gutrune passes.

ACT III, SCENE 1 (45 minutes): During late afternoon in the forest, swimming near a mossy bank, the Rhinemaidens call upon the sun to guide Siegfried to them, since he alone can return their lost gold. Heralded by his horn call, Siegfried appears, momentarily separated from the hunting party. The maidens tease him in the hope of regaining the Ring. He is tempted to give the treasure to them, but when they tell him of Alberich's curse, he keeps the Ring to prove he is not afraid.

No sooner do the Rhinemaidens swim away, predicting his death, than Hagen, Gunther and the other hunters catch up with Siegfried. As the men rest amid shady trees, weary from the chase, drinking wine, Siegfried, prompted by Hagen, reminisces about his youth, describing his adoption by Mime, the repair of the sword, the fight with the dragon and the song of the Forest Bird. Midway in this narrative, Hagen offers the hero wine—an antidote to the magic potion of forgetfulness. Siegfried, his memory restored, continues his tale and rapturously describes the winning of Brünnhilde. Two ravens, messengers to Wotan, fly out of a bush across the Rhine, and as Siegfried turns to watch them, Hagen stabs him in the back with his spear, proclaiming vengeance and justice. As evening falls, Gunther and the other grieving men surround the stricken hero, whose dying thoughts are of Brünnhilde, whom he imagines smiling and calling to him. The vassals bear away Siegfried's body on his shield.

SCENE 2 (36 minutes): At the Gibichung hall, Gutrune wakes from bad dreams, wondering what has happened to Siegfried. She has been frightened by Grane's neighing and Brünnhilde's wild laughter. Hagen returns and tells her Siegfried has been fatally gored by a boar. When the hero's body is carried in, however, she understands the truth, accusing Gunther of murder. He blurts out that Hagen is guilty of the crime. Gunther and Hagen quickly come to blows over the Ring on Siegfried's finger, and Gunther too is savagely killed. As Hagen reaches for the Ring, however, the lifeless Siegfried's arm rises menacingly, causing terror among the Gibichungs.

Like a priestess, beyond earthly pain, Brünnhilde enters, ordering Siegfried's funeral pyre built on the banks of the Rhine. For a time she contemplates the slain hero, eulogizing his purity of heart, even in error. She calls upon the gods to hear her lament, since they too face doom. Taking the Ring from Siegfried's hand, she promises the Rhinemaidens they can reclaim their treasure from her ashes. Then she sends Wotan's ravens homeward with instructions to fly past the Valkyries' rock and dispatch Loge to Valhalla to burn the fortress. Throwing a torch on the funeral pyre, Brünnhilde mounts Grane and rides into the flames, ecstatically greeting Siegfried in death. The Rhine overflows during the conflagration, and Hagen plunges into its waters to seize the Ring, only to be pulled under by the Rhinemaidens. At last the gold has been restored to the Rhine. As Valhalla blazes in the distance, the old order passes and, purified by Brünnhilde's sacrifice, a new era begins.

Götterdämmerung, Act II: after accusing Siegfried of fraud, Brünnhilde (Hildegard Behrens) grasps Hagen's spear to swear to the assembled Gibichungs that her allegations are true

---

Gerald Fitzgerald joined the editorial staff of OPERA NEWS in 1956, John W. Freeman in 1960. The former is co-author with John Ardoin of Callas *(Holt, Rinehart and Winston), the latter is author of* The Metropolitan Opera: Stories of the Great Operas *(Norton).*

WHO WAS WHO IN *DER RING DES NIBELUNGEN* AT THE MET

Compiled by Gerald Fitzgerald and Jean Seward Uppman

Brünnhilde: Amalie Materna (W84-85); Lilli Lehmann (W85-99, SG87-99); Fanny Moran-Olden (WS88-89); Anna Marie Bauman-Triloff (W88-89); Antonia Mielke (WSG90-91); Marie Brema (W95-00, G98-99); Nellie Melba (S96-97); Félia Litvinne (S96-97); Georgine Von Januschowsky (S96-97, G03-04); Lillian Nordica (WSG98-06); Milka Ternina (WSG99-04); Lucienne Bréval (W00-02); Luise Reuss-Belce (W01-02); Johanna Gadski (WS03-17, G03-14); Marion Weed (W03-04, S03-06); Katherine Senger-Bettaque (WS04-05); Edyth Walker (W04-06); Aino Ackté (S04-05); Olive Fremstad (S05-12, G08-14, W10-13); Katherine Fleischer-Edel (S06-07); Martha Leffler-Burckhard (WG07-08); Félicie Kaschowska (W08-09); Berta Morena (S08-12, G24-25); Lucy Weidt (WS10-11); Margarete Matzenauer (W11-29, S13-14); Melanie Kurt (W14-15, SG14-17); Julia Claussen (W21-30); Karin Branzell (W23-24); Nanny Larsén-Todsen (WSG24-27); Florence Easton (S23-28, W26-36); Gertrude Kappel (WG27-35, S27-36); Elena Rakowska (S27-29); Dorothee Manski (W29-30, S32-33); Elisabeth Ohms (W29-32, SG29-31); Göta Ljungberg (W31-35, S31-32, G31-33); Frida Leider (WSG32-34); Anny Konetzni (WS34-35); Kirsten Flagstad (WG34-51, S36-51); Marjorie Lawrence (WSG35-41); Gertrud Rünger (WG36-37); Helen Traubel (W41-51, G41-52, S42-51); Astrid Varnay (W41-54, S46-51, G51-52); Elisabeth Rethberg (S41-42); Jeanne Palmer (W44-45); Helena Braun (W49-50); Margaret Harshaw (G51-62, W53-62, S56-62); Martha Mödl (W56-60, SG56-57); Birgit Nilsson (W59-75, SG61-75); Anita Välkki (W61-65); Gladys Kuchta (G63-64); Régine Crespin (W67-69); Ursula Schröder-Feinen (S72-73); Rita Hunter (W72-77, G73-74); Berit Lindholm (WSG74-75); Elisabeth Payer (S81-82); Janice Yoes (S81-82); Gwyneth Jones (W82-83); Eszter Kovacs (W82-84); Ute Vinzing (W83-84); Hildegard Behrens (W83-89, S87-89, G88-89); Jeannine Altmeyer (W86-88, G88-89); Johanna Meier (W86-89); Linda Kelm (S87-88)

Siegmund: Anton Schott (84-87); Albert Stritt (85-86); Albert Niemann (86-88); Julius Perotti (88-90); Paul Kalisch (88-90); Heinrich Vogl (89-90); Heinrich Gudehus (90-91); Adolph Wallnöfer (95-96); Ernest Van Dyck (98-02); Andreas Dippel (98-08); Georg Anthes (02-09); Alois Burgstaller (02-09); Ernst Kraus (03-04); Carl Burrian (07-13); Erik Schmedes (08-09); Walter Hyde (09-10); Carl Jörn (10-14); Heinrich Hensel (11-12); Jacques Urlus (12-17); Rudolf Berger (13-15); Johannes Sembach (14-22); Morgan Kingston (21-22); Curt Taucher (22-27); Rudolf Laubenthal (23-32); Lauritz Melchior (25-50); Walter Kirchhoff (26-31); Max Lorenz (31-50); Gustaaf De Loor (32-33); Paul Althouse

(33-38); Carl Hartmann (37-38); Eyvind Laholm (39-40); Arthur Carron (42-43); Emery Darcy (44-45); Torsten Ralf (45-47); Set Svanholm (46-54); Günther Treptow (50-51); Wolfgang Windgassen (56-57); Ramon Vinay (56-58); Albert Da Costa (57-58); Jon Vickers (59-84); Karl Liebl (59-60); James King (68-77); Helge Brilioth (72-73); Jess Thomas (72-73); Kolbjörn Höiseth (74-75); Manfred Jung (82-83); Gerd Brenneis (82-83); Peter Hofmann (86-88); Timothy Jenkins (86-88); Gary Lakes (87-89); Robert Schunk (88-89)

Sieglinde: Auguste Seidl-Kraus (84-88); Anna Slach (84-86); Lilli Lehmann (88-99); Katherine Senger-Bettaque (88-89); Félicie Kaschowska (88-90); Sophie Wiesner (89-90); Marie Jahn (90-91); Pauline Schöller-Haag (90-91); Lola Beeth (95-96); Emma Eames (98-05); Susan Strong (99-01); Milka Ternina (99-02); Johanna Gadski (99-17); Luise Reuss-Belce (01-02); Olive Fremstad (03-14); Berta Morena (07-12); Jane Osborn-Hannah (09-10); Melanie Kurt (14-17); Maude Fay (15-16); Maria Jeritza (21-29); Florence Easton (21-29); Elisabeth Rethberg (22-39); Delia Reinhardt (22-24); Maria Müller (24-35); Grete Stückgold (28-34); Gertrude Kappel (29-36); Dorothee Manski (30-32); Elisabeth Ohms (30-31); Göta Ljungberg (31-35); Lotte Lehmann (33-43); Kirsten Flagstad (34-41); Irene Jessner (38-39); Helen Traubel (39-41); Marjorie Lawrence (39-41); Rose Bampton (40-50); Astrid Varnay (41-54); Ella Flesch (44-45); Polyna Stoska (47-49); Regina Resnik (49-50); Margaret Harshaw (53-54); Marianne Schech (56-58); Inge Borkh (57-58); Aase Nordmo-Lövberg (59-60); Leonie Rysanek (59-88); Gladys Kuchta (61-65); Régine Crespin (64-69); Gundula Janowitz (67-68); Hildegard Hillebrecht (68-69); Gwyneth Jones (72-73); Birgit Nilsson (74-75); Janis Martin (74-77); Hildegard Behrens (82-83); Johanna Meier (83-87); Jeannine Altmeyer (86-88); Sabine Hass (87-88); Jessye Norman (88-89); Ellen Shade (88-89); Mechthild Gessendorf (88-89)

Siegfried: Max Alvary (S87-89, G88-89); Albert Niemann (G87-88); Paul Kalisch (G88-89); Heinrich Vogl (SG89-90); Heinrich Gudehus (SG90-91); Jean De Reszke (S96-01, G98-01); Andreas Dippel (S98-08, G99-05); Alexander Von Bandrowski (G01-02); Georg Anthes (SG02-09); Alois Burgstaller (S02-08, G02-09); Ernst Kraus (SG03-04); Heinrich Knote (S04-06, G05-06); Carl Burrian (S06-13, G08-13); Erik Schmedes (G08-09); Heinrich Hensel (S11-12); Jacques Urlus (SG12-17); Carl Jörn (S13-14); Rudolf Berger (G13-15); Johannes Sembach (S15-17); Curt Taucher (S23-25, G24-25); Rudolf Laubenthal (S24-33, G24-31); Lauritz Melchior (S25-48, G28-49); Walter Kirchhoff (S26-

27, G26-28); Max Lorenz (S31-32); Gustaaf De Loor (G32-33); Paul Althouse (G36-37); Carl Hartmann (S37-39, G38-39); Set Svanholm (S46-51, G47-52); Wolfgang Windgassen (SG56-57); Ramon Vinay (G56-57); Hans Hopf (S61-62, G61-64); Karl Liebl (G61-64); Jess Thomas (S72-75, G73-75); Helge Brilioth (S72-73, G73-74); Manfred Jung (S81-82); Wolfgang Neumann (S87-88, G88-89); Toni Krämer (S87-89, G88-89); William Johns (SG88-89)

Wotan/Wanderer: Josef Staudigl (W84-86); Emil Fischer (W85-91, S87-89, R88-90); Alois Grienauer (W88-89); Theodore Reichmann (R89-90, WS89-91); Giuseppe Kaschmann (W95-96); Edouard De Reszke (S96-01); Adolph Mühlmann (W98-04, R00-01, S02-04); Anton Van Rooy (RWS98-08); Theodore Bertram (W99-01, R00-01); David Bispham (W00-03); Otto Goritz (W06-08); Fritz Feinhals (W08-09); Walter Soomer (RWS08-11); Clarence Whitehill (W09-30, S09-31); Hermann Weil (R11-17, W11-15, S13-14); Putnam Griswold (W11-13, S11-14); Carl Braun (W12-17, S13-17, R14-15); Paul Bender (W22-23); Michael Bohnen (WS23-32, R24-32); Friedrich Schorr (W23-42, S24-43, R26-41); Ludwig Hofmann (WS32-38, R33-34); Hans Hermann Nissen (RWS38-39); Julius Huehn (W38-44, R41-43, S41-42); Herbert Janssen (S38-49, R43-45, W43-50); Norman Cordon (S44-45); Osie Hawkins (W44-50); Joel Berglund (W45-49, S46-49, R47-48); Ferdinand Frantz (W49-54, S50-51); Hans Hotter (R50-51, W53-54); Otto Edelmann (W56-62, S56-57); Hermann Uhde (R56-57, W56-60); Jerome Hines (W59-65, R61-62); George London (RS61-62, W64-65); Randolph Symonette (WS61-62); Thomas Stewart (W67-75, R68-75, S72-75); Walter Berry (W67-68); Theo Adam (R68-69, W68-88); Hans Sotin (W72-89, RS87-89); Donald McIntyre (R74-82, W74-87, S74-88); Norman Bailey (W76-77); Franz Ferdinand Nentwig (RS81-82, W82-83); Simon Estes (W82-87); Peter Wimberger (W83-84); James Morris (R87-89, WS88-89); Franz Mazura (W87-88)

Fricka: Marianne Brandt (W84-88); Fanny Moran-Olden (R88-01); Hedwig Reil (W88-89); Louise Meisslinger (R88-90, W88-99); Emmy Sonntag-Uhl (W89-90); Charlotte Huhn (W89-90); Marie Ritter-Götze (W90-91); Rosa Olitzka (W95-01); Ernestine Schumann-Heink (W98-07); Marie Brema (R98-00); Lilli Lehmann (R98-99); Susan Strong (R00-01); Luise Reuss-Belce (R01-03, W02-03); Louise Homer (W03-16, R04-05); Olive Fremstad (R03-14); Edyth Walker (W04-05); Louise Kirkby-Lunn (W06-08); Maria Ranzow (W08-31); Marianne Flahaut (W08-11); Félicie Kaschowska (RW08-09); Florence Wickham (W09-12); Mariska Aldrich (R10-11); Margarete Matzenauer (R11-17, W11-30); Sarah Charles-Cahier (W12-13); Lila Robeson (W12-17); Margarete Ober (W13-17); Melanie Kurt (R15-17); Jeanne Gordon (W21-24); Grace Bradley (W21-22); Sigrid Onegin (W23-24); Karin Branzell (W23-44, R26-39); Marion Telva (W23-28); Nanny Larsén-Todsen (R24-27); Kathleen Howard (W26-27); Gertrude Kappel (R27-36); Julia Claussen (W27-32); Doris Doe (W31-36, R32-33); Maria Olszewska (W32-35, R33-34); Kathryn Meisle (W35-38); Kerstin Thorborg (W36-50, R38-48); Gertrud Rünger (R36-37); Enid Szánthó (W37-38); Risë Stevens (W38-40); Blanche Thebom (R44-57, W44-58); Margaret Harshaw (W46-50, R50-51); Martha Lipton (R56-57); Irene Dalis (W57-65, R61-62); Jean Madeira (W57-58); Nell Rankin (W59-60); Mignon Dunn (W61-87, R74-75); Gladys Kriese (W64-65); Christa Ludwig (W67-89, R88-89); Barbro Ericson (W67-68); Josephine Veasey (RW68-69); Anna

Reynolds (R68-75, W74-75); Ruza Baldani (W72-73); Eva Rándova (R81-82); Gwynn Cornell (W82-83); Lorna Myers (W83-84); Brigitte Fassbaender (W86-87); Waltraud Meier (RW87-88); Gail Gilmore (RW87-88); Helga Dernesch (R87-89, W88-89); Hanna Schwarz (R88-89)

Loge: Max Alvary (88-89); Heinrich Vogl (89-90); Ernest Van Dyck (98-02); Georg Anthes (02-03); Alois Burgstaller (03-07); Carl Burrian (07-13); Carl Jörn (13-14); Johannes Sembach (14-17); Curt Taucher (24-25); George Meader (25-26); Walter Kirchhoff (26-31); Rudolf Laubenthal (31-33); Hans Clemens (33-38); René Maison (35-43); Erich Witte (38-39); Paul Althouse (38-40); John Garris (43-45); Max Lorenz (47-48); Set Svanholm (50-51); Ramon Vinay (56-57); Karl Liebl (61-62); Gerhard Stolze (68-69); Glade Peterson (74-75); Kolbjörn Höiseth (74-75); Ragnar Ulfung (81-82); Heinz Zednik (81-82); Siegfried Jerusalem (87-89); Graham Clark (88-89)

Freia: Katherine Senger-Bettaque (88-89); Ida Klein (88-89); Sophie Wiesner (89-90); Marie Engle (98-99); Susan Strong (99-00); Marguerite Marilly (00-03); Fritzi Scheff (00-01); Camille Seygard (03-04); Marion Weed (04-08); Isabelle L'Huillier (08-09); Alma Gluck (09-12); Vera Curtis (12-15); Marie Rappold (15-17); Maria Müller (24-29); Dorothee Manski (29-39); Göta Ljungberg (31-32); Hilda Burke (38-41); Irene Jessner (41-43); Jarmila Novotna (43-51); Astrid Varnay (44-45); Polyna Stoska (47-48); Mariquita Moll (56-57); Heidi Krall (61-62); Simone Mangelsdorff (68-69); Christine Weidinger (74-75); Mary Ellen Pracht (74-75); Ellen Shade (81-89); Mari-Anne Häggander (87-89); Eva Zseller (88-89)

Froh: Albert Mittelhauser (88-90); Andreas Dippel (98-08); Jacques Bars (99-04); Carl Jörn (08-09); Glenn Hall (09-11); Lambert Murphy (11-14); Paul Althouse (14-39); Ralph Errolle (24-26); Max Altglass (26-28); Alfio Tedesco (28-35); Hans Clemens (30-37); Erich Witte (38-39); John Carter (39-40); Emery Darcy (40-48); Kurt Baum (43-44); Brian Sullivan (50-51); James McCracken (56-57); Robert Nagy (61-62); William Olvis (61-62); Donald Grobe (68-69); Rod MacWherter (68-69); Kolbjörn Höiseth (74-75); Douglas Ahlstedt (74-75); Gerd Brenneis (81-82); Timothy Jenkins (81-88); Mark W. Baker (87-89); Edward Cook (88-89); Gary Bachlund (88-89)

Donner: Alois Grienauer (88-89); Jean Doré (88-89); Joseph Arden (89-90); Herman Devriès (98-00); Eugène Dufriche (00-05); Adolph Mühlmann (02-04); Emil Greder (04-05); Tony Franke (05-06); Paul Lange (06-07); Herbert Waterous (07-09); Herbert Witherspoon (09-10); William Hinshaw (10-13); Basil Millspaugh Ruysdael (13-14); Arthur Middleton (14-15); Henri Scott (15-16); Carl Schlegel (16-26); Arnold Gabor (26-39); Fred Patton (27-29); Alfredo Gandolfi (29-31); Arthur Anderson (31-34); Julius Huehn (35-41); Douglas Beattie (38-39); Osie Hawkins (41-51); William Hargrave (44-45); Kenneth Schon (47-48); Arthur Budney (56-57); Norman Mittelmann (61-62); Sherrill Milnes (68-69); William Dooley (74-75); Vern Shinall (81-82); Philip Joll (87-88); James Courtney (87-89); Gregg Baker (88-89)

Erda: Marianne Brandt (S87-88); Hedwig Reil (RS88-89); Emmy Miron (R88-89); Louise Meisslinger (S88-99, R98-99); Charlotte Huhn (RS89-90); Marie Ritter-Götz (S90-91); Rosa Olitzka (S96-00); Ernestine Schumann-Heink (RS98-32); Louise Kirkby-Lunn (S02-08, R07-08); Marie Maurer

(S02-03); Louise Homer (S03-17, R04-17); Edyth Walker (R03-05, S03-04); Johanna Pöhlmann (R03-04); Josephine Jacoby (S04-06, R05-06); Anna Meitschik (R09-10); Margarete Matzenauer (S11-24); Margarete Ober (RS13-17); Karin Branzell (S23-51, R24-51); Marion Telva (S24-27), R26-27); Maria Ranzow (S30-31); Doris Doe (S31-38, R35-39); Maria Olszewska (RS32-35); Kathryn Meisle (S35-38, R36-37); Kerstin Thorborg (S36-49); Anna Kaskas (R37-38, S38-39); Enid Szánthó (R38-39); Risë Stevens (RS38-39); Christine Johnson (R43-44); Margaret Harshaw (R44-45, S46-49); Claramae Turner (S46-47); Blanche Thebom (R47-48); Jean Madeira (R50-62, S56-62); Sandra Warfield (S56-57); Lili Chookasian (R68-75, S72-75); Ruza Baldani (S72-73); Maureen Forrester (RS74-75); Birgit Finnilä (RS81-82); Jocelyne Taillon (RS81-82); Anne Gjevang (RS87-88); Gweneth Bean (S87-89, R88-89); Birgitta Svendén (RS88-89)

Fafner: Johannes Elmblad (S87-03, R02-03); Eugene Weiss (RS88-89); Conrad Behrens (R89-90, S89-91); Edward Schlömann (R89-90); Armand Castelmary (S96-97); Lodovico Viviani (S96-97); Lampriere Pringle (RS98-00); Marcel Journet (R00-04, S03-04); Robert Blass (S00-10, R01-10); Victor Klöpfer (S03-04); Allen Hinckley (S08-09); Basil Millspaugh Ruysdael (RS10-17); Carl Braun (R13-14); William Gustafson (S23-31); James Wolfe (R24-39, S26-32); Adamo Didur (R25-27); Siegfried Tappolet (S30-33); Emanuel List (S33-47, R35-45); Chase Baromeo (S35-36); Norman Cordon (S37-39); Herbert Alsen (S38-39); Douglas Beattie (R38-39); Dezsö Ernster (S46-51, R50-57); Mihály Székely (S46-47, R47-48); Luben Vichey (S48-49); Kurt Böhme (S56-57); Ernst Wiemann (R61-62); Gottlob Frick (RS61-62); Karl Ridderbusch (R68-69); Hans Sotin (S72-73); John Macurdy (S72-89, R74-75); Aage Haugland (R81-89, S81-82); Matti Salminen (RS88-89)

Fasolt: Ludwig Mödlinger (88-89); Edward Schlömann (89-90); Conrad Behrens (89-90); Adolph Mühlmann (98-10); Robert Blass (00-04); Victor Klöpfer (03-04); Emil Greder (04-05); Herbert Witherspoon (10-15); Putnam Griswold (11-12); Carl Braun (15-17); Léon Rothier (24-30); Siegfried Tappolet (30-33); Emanuel List (33-39); Ludwig Hofmann (35-38); Norman Cordon (36-43); Herbert Alsen (38-39); Alexander Kipnis (40-41); Nicola Moscona (43-45); Jerome Hines (47-62); Kurt Böhme (56-57); Ernst Wiemann (61-62); Martti Talvela (68-69); Bengt Rundgren (74-75); John Macurdy (81-89); Gwynne Howell (88-89); Jan-Hendrik Rootering (88-89)

Alberich: Joseph Beck (RS88-90), Rudolph Von Milde (SG87-88); Alois Grienauer (R88-89); Ludwig Mödlinger (S88-89); Juan Luria (S90-91); David Bispham (S96-03, RG98-03); Fritz Friedrichs (RSG99-00); Otto Goritz (RS03-17, G08-15); Adolph Mühlmann (S01-02, R04-05); Robert Leonhardt (S14-15); Gustav Schützendorf (S23-35, RG24-35); Arnold Gabor (G30-39, RS38-39); Eduard Habich (RSG35-37); Adolf Vogel (RSG37-39); Walter Olitzki (R39-43, S39-47, G39-46); Frederick Lechner (RG43-45, S43-47); Gerhard Pechner (R47-57, S47-62, G47-64); Lawrence Davidson (R50-57, G50-64, S56-57); Alois Pernerstorfer (G51-52); Ralph Herbert (RSG61-62); Zoltán Kelemen (R68-69); Gustav Neidlinger (S72-73); Russell Christopher (S72-73); Marius Rintzler (G73-75, RS74-75); Andrew Foldi (RSG74-75); Franz Mazura (RS81-89, G88-89); Jozsef Dene (RS81-82); Julian Patrick (R87-89, G88-89); Ekkehard Wlaschiha (S87-89, RG88-89)

Mime: T. Ferenczy (S87-88); Otto Kemlitz (S87-91); Wilhelm Sedlmayer (RS88-89); Paul Kalisch (R89-90); Nicolai Gorski (S89-90); Adolph Von Hübbenet (S96-01, R00-01); Hans Meffert (RS98-99); Hans Breuer (RS99-00); Albert Reiss (RS01-17); George Meader (S23-31, R24-31); Max Bloch (S24-30, R25-26); Hans Clemens (S31-32); Marek Windheim (R31-36, S32-36); Karl Laufkötter (RS36-45); Erich Witte (S38-39); John Garris (S46-49, R47-48); Peter Klein (RS50-51); Leslie Chabay (RS50-51); Norman Kelley (RS56-57); Paul Kuen (RS61-62); Andrea Velis (R68-69); Gerhard Stolze (S72-73); Ragnar Ulfung (S72-82, R74-82); Heinz Zednik (RS81-82); Horst Hiestermann (RS87-89); Paul Crook (R87-88); Graham Clark (R87-89, S88-89); Hubert Delamboye (S87-88, R88-89)

Hunding: Joseph Kögel (84-85); Phillip Lehmler (85-86); Georg Sieglitz (86-87); Johannes Elmblad (87-03); Eugene Weiss (88-89); Conrad Behrens (89-91); Mr. Bucha (95-96); Lampriere Pringle (98-00); David Bispham (98-99); Robert Blass (00-10); Victor Klöpfer (03-04); Allen Hinckley (08-11); Basil Millspaugh Ruysdael (10-17); Henri Scott (15-17); William Gustafson (21-31); Paul Bender (22-27); Michael Bohnen (25-28); Pavel Ludikar (26-28); Richard Mayr (27-30); Ivar Andresen (30-31); Siegfried Tappolet (30-33); Carlton Gauld (31-32); Emanuel List (33-50); Ludwig Hofmann (37-38); Herbert Alsen (38-39); Norman Cordon (39-46); Alexander Kipnis (41-46); Mihály Székely (46-50); Nicola Moscona (46-47); Dezsö Ernster (47-60); Luben Vichey (48-54); Hans Hotter (53-54); Kurt Böhme (56-57); William Wildermann (57-60); Ernst Wiemann (61-65); Gottlob Frick (61-62); David Ward (64-65); Karl Ridderbusch (67-69); John Macurdy (67-88); Martti Talvela (68-69); Hans Sotin (72-73); Bengt Rundgren (74-75); Manfred Schenk (76-77); Hans Tschammer (82-83); Aage Haugland (82-88); Siegfried Vogel (86-87); Matti Salminen (88-89); Kurt Moll (88-89)

Forest Bird: Auguste Seidl-Kraus (87-88); Sophie Traubmann (88-02); Betty Frank (89-90); Jennie Broch (90-91); Mina Schilling (96-97); Marie Engle (98-99); Olga Pevny (99-00); Suzanne Adams (99-00); Fritzi Scheff (00-03); Camille Seygard (01-03); Marguerite Lemon (03-05); Bella Alten (04-14); Marie Rappold (06-07); Lenora Sparkes (08-17); Elisabeth Schumann (14-15); Edith Mason (15-17); Thalia Sabanieeva (23-32); Charlotte Ryan (23-26); Elisabeth Kandt (25-26); Editha Fleischer (26-36); Helen Gleason (35-36); Stella Andreva (36-37); Marita Farell (37-38); Natalie Bodanya (37-41); Eleanor Steber (40-41); Nadine Conner (41-48); Mimi Benzell (46-47); Paula Lenchner (47-49); Erna Berger (50-51); Genevieve Warner (50-51); Laurel Hurley (56-57); Martina Arroyo (61-62); Judith Blegen (72-73); Betsy Norden (74-82); Gwendolyn Bradley (81-88); Dawn Upshaw (87-89)

Hagen: Emil Fischer (87-91); Edouard De Reszke (98-03); Robert Blass (00-08); Allen Hinckley (08-14); Leon Rains (08-09); Putnam Griswold (11-13); Carl Braun (12-17); Basil Millspaugh Ruysdael (13-14); Michael Bohnen (24-32); Siegfried Tappolet (29-31); Ludwig Hofmann (32-38); Emanuel List (33-46); Alexander Kipnis (39-46); Dezsö Ernster (47-64); Kurt Böhme (56-57); Ernst Wiemann (61-64); Gottlob Frick (61-62); Bengt Rundgren (73-75); John Macurdy (74-89); Matti Salminen (88-89)

Günther: Adolf Robinson (87-89); Joseph Beck (88-90); Alois Grienauer (88-89); Juan Luria (90-91); Adolph

Mühlmann (98-09); Clarence Whitehill (09-32); Walter Soomer (10-11); Hermann Weil (11-17); William Hinshaw (12-13); Friedrich Schorr (24-41); Carl Schlegel (24-25); Gustav Schützendorf (30-32); Julius Huehn (36-43); Herbert Janssen (38-51); Osie Hawkins (45-49); Paul Schöffler (51-52); Hans Hotter (51-52); Hermann Uhde (56-57); Norman Mittelmann (61-64); Walter Cassel (61-64); Thomas Stewart (73-74); William Dooley (73-75); Donald McIntyre (74-75); Anthony Raffell (88-89)

Gutrune: Auguste Seidl-Kraus (87-88); Louise Meisslinger (88-90); Ida Klein (89-90); Félicie Kaschowska (89-90); Marie Jahn (90-91); Frances Saville (98-99); Olga Pevny (98-99); Susan Strong (99-01); Luise Reuss-Belce (01-03); Marion Weed (03-08); Rita Fornia (08-14); Jane Osborn-Hannah (09-11); Vera Curtis (14-15); Julia Heinrich (15-16); Marie Sundelius (16-17); Maria Müller (24-30); Charlotte Ryan (24-25); Editha Fleischer (26-35); Marcella Röseler (26-27); Dorothee Manski (29-39); Irene Jessner (36-52); Astrid Varnay (43-46); Polyna Stoska (47-49); Regina Resnik (50-52); Marianne Schech (56-57); Ingrid Bjoner (61-62); Gladys Kuchta (61-62); Heidi Krall (6l-62); Mary Curtis-Verna (63-64); Frances Yeend (63-64); Nell Rankin (73-75); Mary Ellen Pracht (73-74); Kathryn Harries (88-89)

Waltraute (Götterdämmerung): Ernestine Schumann-Heink (98-07); Louise Meisslinger (98-99); Louise Homer (02-16); Edyth Walker (04-06); Margarete Matzenauer (11-16); Margarete Ober (13-17); Karin Branzell (24-42); Marion Telva (24-25); Maria Ranzow (30-31); Doris Doe (31-36); Maria Olszewska (32-35); Kathryn Meisle (35-36); Kerstin Thorborg (38-49); Blanche Thebom (44-57); Margaret Harshaw (48-52); Elisabeth Höngen (51-52); Jean Madeira (56-62); Irene Dalis (61-64); Rita Gorr (63-64); Mignon Dunn (63-75); Anna Reynolds (74-75); Christa Ludwig (88-89); Helga Dernesch (88-89)

Conductor: Leopold Damrosch (W84-85); Walter Damrosch+ (W84-02, RSG00-02); John Lund (W84-85); Anton Seidl+ (W85-96, S87-97, G87-91, R88-90); Franz Schalk+ (RWSG98-99); Emil Paur+ (RWSG99-00); Philippe Flon (W01-02); Alfred Hertz+ (RWSG02-15); Felix Mottl (WS03-04); Gustav Mahler (WS07-08); Arturo Toscanini (G08-09); Artur Bodanzky+ (RWSG15-39); Paul Eisler (S16-17); Tullio Serafin (S27-29); Giuseppe Bamboschek (W27-28); Joseph Rosenstock (W29-30, G63-64); Karl Riedel (W29-33, RG35-36); Erich Leinsdorf+ (W37-77, RS38-82, G39-62); George Szell+ (RWS43-45, G43-46); Paul Breisach (W44-46); Fritz Stiedry+ (W46-58, S46-57, RG47-57); Dimitri Mitropoulos (W56-57); Karl Böhm (W59-60); William Steinberg (W64-65); Herbert Von Karajan (W67-69, R68-69); Berislav Klobucar (W67-68); Rafael Kubelik (G73-74); Sixten Ehrling+ (RWSG74-75); Silvio Varviso (W82-83); James Levine+ (W83-89, RS87-89, G88-89); Richard Woitach (W83-84); Max Epstein (W87-88)

Das Rheingold: 51 seasons/130 performances (84 MOH, 29 MOL, 17 E); #1/4/89 (9 MOH, 7 E), 2/21/90 (3 MOH), #1/12/99 (4 MOH), 2/6/00 (MOH, 1 E), 11/26/00 (2 MOH, 2 E), 2/24/02 (1 MOH, 1 E), 1/14/03 (2 MOH, 1 E), #3/3/04 (2 MOH, 1 E), 1/5/05 (2 MOH), 12/25/05 (2 MOH), 3/19/07 (1 MOH), 4/13/08 (1 MOH), 3/4/09 (1 MOH, 1 E), 1/24/10 (2 MOH), 2/2/11 (1 MOH), 2/1/12 (1 MOH), 1/29/13 (1 MOH), #1/29/14 (1 MOH), 1/28/15 (1 MOH), 2/3/16 (3 MOH), 1/4/17 (2 MOH), 2/26/25 (1 MOH), 2/25/26 (1 MOH), 1/28/27 (3 MOH), 2/24/28 (1 MOH), 2/21/29 (1 MOH), 2/21/30 (1

MOH), 2/20/31 (1 MOH), 2/26/32 (1 MOH), 1/27/33 (1 MOH), 2/16/34 (1 MOH), 2/8/35 (1 MOH), 2/6/36 (2 MOH), 2/9/37 (2 MOH, 1 E), 2/9/38 (1 MOH, 1 E), 1/3/39 (3 MOH, 1 E), 2/2/40 (2 MOH), 2/7/41 (1 MOH), 1/22/42 (1 MOH), 2/9/43 (1 MOH), 2/8/44 (2 MOH), 2/2/45 (2 MOH), #1/7/48 (2 MOH), 1/25/51 (2 MOH), 1/18/57 (3 MOH), 12/16/61 (3 MOH), #11/22/68 (5 MOL), 2/10/75 (3 MOL), 9/22/81 (4 MOL), #10/9/87 (8 MOL), 9/28/88 (9 MOL)

Die Walküre: 73 seasons/468 performances (290 MOH, 62 MOL, 116 E); #1/30/85 (7 MOH, 6 E), 11/30/85 (4 MOH, 3 E), 11/10/86 (3 MOH), 1/18/88 (4 MOH), 2/15/89 (4 MOH, 6 E), 2/12/90 (3 MOH, 1 E), 2/6/91 (4 MOH), #1/9/96 (2 MOH), 11/18/98 (7 MOH, 7 E), 11/24/99 (6 MOH, 4 E), 11/27/00 (5 MOH, 5 E), 11/15/01 (3 MOH, 4 E), 1/16/03 (3 MOH, 3 E), #11/25/03 (5 MOH, 4 E), 12/17/04 (4 MOH), 12/9/05 (3 MOH, 3 E), 2/26/07 (2 MOH, 1 E), 2/7/08 (4 MOH, 4 E), 11/18/08 (5 MOH, 3 E), 1/8/10 (4 MOH, 3 E), 11/18/10 (5 MOH), 2/8/12 (5 MOH, 1 E), 12/14/12 (6 MOH, 1 E), #12/20/13 (7 MOH, 1 E), 12/11/14 (7 MOH, 1 E), 12/16/15 (5 MOH), 2/8/17 (4 MOH, 1 E), 12/16/21 (6 MOH, 2 E), 11/23/22 (4 MOH, 2 E), 12/20/23 (6 MOH, 1 E), 1/21/25 (4 MOH, 1 E), 1/7/26 (5 MOH, 1 E), 12/8/26 (5 MOH, 1 E), 12/14/27 (4 MOH, 1 E), 11/27/28 (6 MOH, 1 E), 11/9/29 (7 MOH, 2 E), 10/29/30 (7 MOH, 1 E), 11/14/31 (6 MOH, 2 E), 12/6/32 (3 MOH, 1 E), 12/29/33 (4 MOH, 2 E), 12/26/34 (5 MOH, 2 E), #12/18/35 (4 MOH, 1 E), 12/21/36 (6 MOH, 4 E), 12/18/37 (7 MOH, 1 E), 11/23/38 (6 MOH, 4 E), 12/6/39 (7 MOH, 3 E), 12/4/40 (4 MOH, 2 E), 12/6/41 (3 MOH, 1 E), 2/16/43 (3 MOH, 1 E), 12/2/43 (4 MOH, 1 E), 12/2/44 (5 MOH, 2 E), 1/25/46 (2 MOH, 3 E), 12/5/46 (5 MOH), #1/13/48 (3 MOH, 2 E), 12/29/48 (4 MOH), 12/12/49 (5 MOH, 1 E), 2/1/51 (2 MOH), 2/4/54 (4 MOH), 1/22/57 (4 MOH, 1 E), 2/5/58 (4 MOH), 2/9/60 (5 MOH), 12/23/61 (4 MOH), 2/22/65 (6 MOH), #11/21/67 (9 MOL), 10/31/68 (5 MOL), 11/24/72 (5 MOL), 2/20/75 (6 MOL), 1/28/77 (7 MOL), 3/17/83 (5 MOL), 4/26/84 (9 E), #9/22/86 (10 MOL), 10/24/87 (9 MOL), 3/24/89 (6 MOL)

Siegfried: 57 seasons/237 performances (166 MOH, 23 MOL, 48 E); #11/9/87 (11 MOH), 12/21/88 (6 MOH, 7 E), 3/17/90 (2 MOH), 1/28/91 (4 MOH), #12/30/96 (7 MOH, 5 E), 12/16/98 (4 MOH), 2/13/00 (2 MOH, 1 E), 11/28/00 (2 MOH, 2 E), 3/4/02 (1 MOH, 1 E), 1/19/03 (3 MOH, 5 E), #1/18/04 (3 MOH, 3 E), 1/19/05 (1 MOH, 1 E), 12/13/05 (3 MOH, 1 E), 12/29/06 (4 MOH, 1 E), 2/19/08 (4 MOH, 1 E), 3/18/09 (2 MOH, 1 E), 12/16/09 (3 MOH), 1/14/11 (2 MOH), †12/30/11 (3 MOH, 2 E), 1/17/13 (2 MOH), #12/4/13 (4 MOH), 1/9/15 (3 MOH), 1/15/16 (4 MOH), 12/26/16 (5 MOH, 2 E), 2/2/24 (2 MOH), 3/11/25 (2 MOH, 1 E), 3/10/26 (2 MOH), 2/10/27 (3 MOH, 2 E), 2/18/28 (4 MOH, 1 E), 2/7/29 (3 MOH, 1 E), 3/7/30 (2 MOH), 12/11/30 (5 MOH, 1 E), 1/15/32 (3 MOH, 1 E), 1/17/33 (2 MOH, 1 E), 1/24/34 (2 MOH), 12/28/34 (3 MOH), †1/3/36 (3 MOH), 1/22/37 (4 MOH, 1 E), 12/3/37 (5 MOH, 1 E), 11/28/38 (6 MOH, 1 E), 2/6/40 (2 MOH, 1 E), 1/10/41 (3 MOH), 2/6/42 (2 MOH), 3/2/43 (1 MOH), 2/22/44 (2 MOH), 2/13/45 (2 MOH), 11/15/46 (4 MOH, 1 E), #1/21/48 (2 MOH, 1 E), 1/14/49 (3 MOH, 1 E), 2/7/51 (3 MOH), 1/30/57 (3 MOH), 1/2/62 (3 MOH), #11/17/72 (5 MOL), 3/5/75 (3 MOL), 9/24/81 (6 MOL), #2/12/88 (6 MOL), 4/15/89 (3 MOL)

Götterdämmerung: 55 seasons/206 performances (156 MOH, 19 MOL, 31 E); #1/25/88 (7 MOH), 3/11/89 (4 MOH, 7 E), 2/7/90 (5 MOH), 2/13/91 (4 MOH), #1/24/99 (4 MOH), 2/15/00 (2 MOH, 1 E), 11/30/00 (3 MOH, 2 E), 3/6/02 (1

MOH, 1 E), 1/23/03 (2 MOH, 3 E), #3/10/04 (2 MOH, 4 E), 1/26/05 (2 MOH), 12/22/05 (3 MOH, 1 E), 3/27/07 (1 MOH), 4/18/08 (1 MOH), 12/10/08 (5 MOH, 2 E), 2/1/10 (2 MOH), 2/22/11 (1 MOH), 11/23/11 (3 MOH, 1 E), 11/16/12 (4 MOH), #2/19/14 (3 MOH), 2/18/15 (2 MOH), 11/18/15 (3 MOH), 2/22/17 (1 MOH), 1/31/25 (4 MOH), 3/19/26 (2 MOH), 1/14/27 (4 MOH), 1/26/28 (3 MOH), 1/12/29 (2 MOH), 1/17/30 (3 MOH), 1/16/31 (4 MOH, 1 E), 3/17/32 (2 MOH, 1 E), 11/24/32 (4 MOH), 3/9/34 (2 MOH, 1 E), 1/25/35 (2 MOH), 1/11/36 (4 MOH), 3/2/37 (2 MOH, 1 E), 3/1/38 (3 MOH), 12/12/38 (4 MOH, 1 E), 1/25/40 (3 MOH, 1 E), 1/29/41 (4 MOH), 2/12/42 (2 MOH, 1 E), 11/25/42 (3 MOH), 2/29/44 (2 MOH), 12/8/44 (3 MOH, 1 E), 2/11/46 (3 MOH), #1/29/48 (2 MOH), 12/2/48 (4 MOH, 1 E), 2/15/51 (2 MOH), 12/13/51 (5 MOH), 2/7/57 (4 MOH), 12/9/61 (5 MOH), 11/14/63 (4 MOH), #3/8/74 (7 MOL), 3/21/75 (3 MOL), #10/21/88 (9 MOL)

R—*Das Rheingold*; W—*Die Walküre*; S—*Siegfried*; G—*Götterdämmerung*; MOH—old Metropolitan Opera House; MOL—new Metropolitan Opera House; E—elsewhere in New York or on tour; + conducted complete cycle; ≠ new production; † revised production

THE RING — METROPOLITAN OPERA

Editors/GERALD FITZGERALD, PATRICK O'CONNOR
Design/GREGORY DOWNER
Production/JEFFREY HILDT   Publisher/G. PALMER LeROY
assisted by other members of the OPERA NEWS staff:
Jane L. Poole, Managing Editor   John W. Freeman, Associate Editor
Brian Kellow, Assistant Editor   Marylis Sevilla-Gonzaga, Assistant Editor   Lorraine Rosenfeld, Editorial Assistant
Elizabeth Diggans, Assistant Art Director   Donatella Spina, Advertising Assistant
Kristina Michelsen, Production Assistant
Jean Seward Uppman, Special Editorial Attaché   Louise Bloomfield, Editorial Consultant

PICTURE SOURCES

TITLE PAGES
© Beth Bergman 1988 (Alberich with Rhinegold); © Johan Elbers 1988 (gods with rainbow bridge)

FORGERS OF THE *RING*
© Bill Hayward 1988

THE EVOLUTION OF THE *RING*
Richard Wagner Gedenkstätte, Bayreuth (Wagner in silks); Harvard College Library, Theatre Collection (Damrosch); Metropolitan Opera Archives (1885 *Walküre* program); Festspielhaus Archiv, Bayreuth (Ludwig II)

LEITMOTIF AND MEANING
Festspielhaus Archiv, Bayreuth (auditorium seats); Harvard College Library, Theatre Collection (Beck); Metropolitan Opera Archives (Niemann, Nordica, 1887 *Siegfried* program, 1888 *Götterdämmerung* program); courtesy of Robert Tuggle (Jean De Reszke, Edouard De Reszke, Van Dyck, Van Rooy); Culver Pictures, Inc. (Bispham, 1890 *Illustrated American*); courtesy of Girvice Archer, Jr. (Materna)

WAGNER AS POET
Richard Wagner Gedenkstätte, Bayreuth (Wagner in chair); courtesy of Robert Tuggle (Urlus, Reiss, Burgstaller, Fremstad, Homer, Hinckley); Culver Pictures, Inc. (Matzenauer, Griswold, Jörn, Rappold); Metropolitan Opera Archives (Weil, Kurt, Sembach); Echt Foto (Breker sculpture)

GODS, DEMIGODS AND MORTALS
Courtesy of Rolf Langenfass (costume designs)

The son of the Metropolitan Opera's original Siegfried, Max Alvary, costumed as baby Siegfried, 1887

DAS RHEINGOLD COLOR FOLIO
© Beatriz Schiller 1988 (Wotan with Ring; Rhinemaidens; entrance of Loge); © Erika Davidson 1988 (Fricka with Loge and Donner); © Beth Bergman 1988 (Alberich with Wotan; Fasolt with Freia)

RING TALES
The Bettmann Archive (Nietzsche); Museum of the City of New York (Materna); Metropolitan Opera Archives (1913-14 Kautsky production, Schorr, Branzell, Bohnen, Melchior as Siegmund, Leider, List, Maison, Stevens, Thorborg, Traubel, Resnik, Klein, Vinay); Culver Pictures, Inc. (Shaw, Seidl-Kraus with Seidl, Whitehill, Taucher); Festspielhaus Archiv, Bayreuth (Cosima Wagner); courtesy of Peggy Tueller (Nilsson)

DIE WALKÜRE COLOR FOLIO
© Beatriz Schiller 1988 (Brünnhilde); © William Harris/Education Department, Metropolitan Opera Guild 1988 (Siegmund with Sieglinde; Act II Brünnhilde with Wotan); © Erika Davidson 1988 (the Valkyries); © Johan Elbers 1988 (Act III Wotan with Brünnhilde)

SIEGFRIED COLOR FOLIO
© Beatriz Schiller 1988 (Siegfried forging; Erda; Siegfried with the Wanderer); © Johan Elbers 1988 (Mime with the Wanderer; Alberich with Mime; Brünnhilde)

THE RING: 100 YEARS AT THE MET
Metropolitan Opera Archives (Bodanzky, 1947-48 Simonson production *Siegfried* Act I, Act III, Scene 2, and *Götterdämmerung* Act II, Dunn, Stewart, Milnes, Thomas)

A *RING* BOOKSHELF
© Henry Grossman 1988 (Karajan); © E. Fred Sher 1988 (Schneider-Siemssen production *Rheingold* Scenes 1 and 4, *Walküre* Act III); © Beth Bergman 1988 (*Walküre* Act I, *Siegfried* Acts I and II, *Götterdämmerung* Act I, Scene 1, and Act II); Ilse Buhs (Leinsdorf)

GÖTTERDÄMMERUNG COLOR FOLIO
© Johan Elbers 1988 (Siegfried with Brünnhilde; Brünnhilde with flames); © Beth Bergman 1988 (Act I, Scene 1; Act II; Act III, Scene 1); © Beatriz Schiller 1988 (Waltraute with Brünnhilde)

STORIES OF THE MUSIC DRAMAS
All photographs © Beth Bergman 1988 with one exception: Winnie Klotz/Metropolitan Opera (Gunther with Gutrune)

Other illustrations from the files of OPERA NEWS, Metropolitan Opera Guild

For additional copies of *The Ring—Metropolitan Opera*, send $11 (postage and handling included) to Metropolitan Opera Guild, 1865 Broadway, New York, N.Y. 10023